Something for
the weekend?

Something for
the weekend?

*Twenty cars in twenty-five years – and
each with a story*

Alwyn Brice

To order additional copies of this book, contact:
Xlibris Corporation
0-800-644-6988
www.xlibrispublishing.co.uk
Orders@Xlibris.co.uk
300571

CONTENTS

PREFACE

Why buy a book that charts the buying and selling of an individual's cars over a span of 25 years?

A good question.

After all, this volume is not only extremely personal, it is all about whim and wisdom (although not in proportional quantity), and the fun and the follies of buying cars that have, in the main, not been mainstream at all. Equally, it's about chance conversations, odd reminiscences and sometimes downright unfathomable behaviour that has seen the author acquire yet another example of what is colloquially referred to these days as a "set of wheels." As his long-suffering wife, Helen, is fond of saying, "I've pushed most of them at some point."

This book is dedicated, then, to her, along with the thousands of other partners out there who willingly (or otherwise) are sucked into that all-devouring Charybdis that is the world of classic car ownership . . .

For Helen, Charles and Emma
(and their tolerance)

ACKNOWLEDGEMENTS

My grateful thanks go to:

Sherilee Clinch and Jason Taylor for the cover design
Tom Sharrad, for the dire task of proofing
Gary & Julie Simpson for Escort memories
Phil Homer of the Standard Motor Club

CHAPTER ONE

Miniature dreams

In the beginning there were no cars at all for the author, himself a product of the baby boom years, who was simply content to play on the carpet with his treasured Matchbox toys, along with a smaller selection of Corgi and Dinky vehicles. These latter were the stuff of Christmases and birthdays, for they were not cheap compared to the 1s (5p in new money) or so that afforded a Lesney product. This continually augmenting fleet was no different from that of any other boy growing up in the late 1950s. And whilst not every hearthrug experience turned its occupant into a car-obsessed collector, I guess that psychiatrists would readily form a link between this early behaviour and that which would manifest itself in later years.

I can't really recall a defining moment in my life when I realised that cars would be a passion for me. I grew up in Norbury, just outside London, and to be quite frank, there weren't many cars at all in our terraced street. I never, from memory, saw anything remotely interesting on my daily walk to school (these, remember, were pre-4x4 school drop-off days with mother at the wheel), aside from a dark green MGBGT that was habitually parked near the playground. It was all rather dull, in fact. My sole reference to that big wide world of the motor car was the *Observers Book of Cars*, the 1965 edition.

I have it still.

An early interest in the automotive world came courtesy of Lesney,
Corgi and Dinky

I was about 10 when we moved to Biggin Hill, in Kent. Since I was approaching the Eleven Plus examination age, somehow my parents managed to keep me on at the London school although I was living in another county. This necessitated a lot of logistical problems that were solved through my father's car, helpful neighbours and, on many occasions, a bus trip to New Addington followed by the best part of 4 miles on foot. No-one batted an eyelid at such behaviour in those carefree, halcyon days and if nothing else, the frequent exercise built up my leg muscles to a degree that would have been envied by Arnold Schwarzenegger.

On the days that I walked over to my father's place of work in Mitcham, I'd spend time in his office, waiting for him to finish work before taking me home. There I'd draw and play with sundry bits and pieces that his engineering company had turned out. A rather benevolent colleague of his, one Charlie Rose, occasionally brought in an old copy of *Motor Sport*, which he passed on to me. I don't think that I ever read much of the content but the pictures were interesting enough, showing scenes from the Monte Carlo Rally and the like. Also of interest were the advertisements for all manner of motoring paraphernalia, notably those of Les Leston. Car-themed cufflinks, string back driving gloves, lapel badges . . . all this fired my imagination.

Shuttling back and forth in the traffic each day in the passenger seat of my father's Dove Grey Austin Cambridge, seatbelt-free, I quickly came to recognise all the cars on the road; in fact, I could tell any car by its tail-light. Admittedly, there were fewer cars about then but even so, there were myriad varieties when it came to lenses, for we were in that glorious pre-computer age when individuality was a fact of life. It was a red letter day when I saw something out of the ordinary. Again, for some reason, I don't ever remember anything exotic doing the Croydon rounds but one evening I espied a Bond Equipe, something I'd never seen before, and it took me a while to find out what it was. The "I-spy Cars" book of the time, a magnet for people like myself, was dutifully filled in although certain vehicles proved highly elusive – in fact, I began to doubt their very existence.

This kind of reading material was to slowly form the habits of my later life

It wasn't all about tail-lights, though, for if it was, I'm quite sure that by now you'd be putting this book down and reaching for a stiff drink. The 1960s was a decade of change, one of throwing caution to the winds and an escape from the lingering effects of the austerity years. It was also a decade of merchandising, as witnessed by any self-respecting filling station. Petrol giveaways were something foisted on every motorist, whether he or she wanted them or not. There was a time (and still is, for aught I know) when every householder in the land had one or more of those free glass tumblers in his kitchen. It didn't stop there: decals from Esso, Regent, BP *et al* were all lapped up. Tiger Tails, Esso oil drop men (and women – for times were liberated), collectors' cards and even models were all churned out to an increasingly mobile consumer base. For my part, I was desirous of an Esso oilman on a chain and I pestered one my father's drivers for an example on the rare occasions that he picked me up from school. I never did get that particular memento until much later on in life.

The same year I recall devoting an inordinate amount of time to a drawing of an E-type Jaguar convertible in my school diary. The car had been pictured in the *Daily Mirror* at that year's Motor Show and I was captivated by its sleek styling and sheer flambuoyance. I've never owned an E-type although I have driven one: it's the kind of car that remains etched on one's memory. So it's interesting to note that my young son, 11 years old at the time of writing, has been a Jaguar devotee for some years—and has an equal admiration for this vehicle.

Around 1964 was the time that I bought my first camera, a simple Hong Kong-made Binaflex product that cost the princely sum of 10s 6d and was made available through collecting some tea tokens from Primo, I think the brand was. My first film, in glorious monochrome, was largely (un)focussed on cars that I saw around the roads of Biggin Hill and included a Triumph Spitfire and a 1950s Lagonda.

Looking back, I guess that the seeds had been sown . . .

CHAPTER TWO

Roadworthy

Between the ages of 11 and 18, my life followed the traditional male adolescent pattern that involved music, females, experimenting with hitherto unknown substances and all manner of other interesting sidelines. I spent a great deal of my time making kits, doubtless a genetic inheritance, since my father had been an engineer and had an acute eye for detail and workmanship. Aircraft, and not cars, were my principal interest during that time although, like all red-blooded males, I had a Scalextric racing car set and devoured periodicals such as *Model Cars* and the *Airfix Magazine*. I never got into the scratch-building side of slot cars that was a hobby of some of my contemporaries in the late 1960s, but I did enjoy building car kits and racing slot cars. On the car kit front, I recall buying the Triumph TR4a, the E-type Jaguar (that car again!) and, for some inexplicable reason, a couple of vintage cars plus an American dragster. I'm not sure why I purchased the latter: my interest was really rooted in British cars of the 1960s by then. I found, however, that to build car kits meant that you'd need to be able to spray the bodywork, since hand-painting just didn't work. As that skill was beyond me, I veered away from cars, preferring instead tanks and soft-skinned vehicles that didn't require such niceties.

As for the real thing, I began to take more interest in what was on the roads. The odd Sunbeam Alpine and Austin Healey lived locally, but there wasn't a huge number of what I'd term interesting vehicles. By 11, I was at grammar school in Bromley and I recall my PE teacher buying a new silver-blue Mk1 Ford Capri, which was something a little different at the time. It looked quite sporty but I knew nothing then about the modest 1300cc engine that lay under the bonnet.

A couple of years later we decamped to Buckinghamshire as my father had been obliged to change his job. A new house, a new school and new friends all followed in due course. My mid-teen years were probably a period of fertile growth insofar as cars were concerned: I found other pupils interested in this subject and we'd pore over car magazines (notably *Custom Car* and *Cars and Car Conversions*) as well as send off for car company brochures. *Cars and Car Conversions* was a real oddity at the time since it carried all manner of bizarre stories about mechanical changes and transformations. Readers would write in about the thorny practicalities of mating a certain gearbox to a certain axle whilst others would be seeking the best way to shoehorn a V8 into something like a Hillman Imp. I well recall one complete lunatic who'd somehow acquired a Merlin aero engine and squeezed it into a Rolls Royce. It seemed a mad thing to do back in the 1970s but upon reflection, he was probably only aping those great pre-war racers who used to attend Brooklands in such outlandish confections.

Kit cars were also in vogue at the time; in particular, the Beach Buggy was gaining a following, although this product of California was rather ill at ease when transposed to the likes of Clapham or Clitheroe. Other types of kit were also being offered, many of which were based on VW running gear. For my money, the only one that merited attention was the stunning ADD Nova, which featured a ram-assisted lift up canopy. It was incredibly striking and looked every inch the jaw-dropper that it was, even if in basic guise it would have run on a humble Beetle 1300cc engine. The black and white factory brochure (which I had) mentioned the wisdom of dropping in a 2.4-litre Porsche engine, the sort of thing that could be picked up at a scrapyard then.

How times have changed . . .

Living near to Newport Pagnell meant that I'd see an Aston Martin every so often; and other cars began to come more into focus. A local businessman owned a delightful black Rolls from the 1930s bearing the distinctive AL 7 registration that I quite fancied; and another chap I knew ran a secondhand car showroom and his transport was a Mercedes 280CE. This he used to fetch me in when I did a spot of baby-sitting for him: it was finished in gold, reeked of Fabergé West and sported the registration UGO 2. A lovely car, with that pillarless design, it led me to start scanning the small ads for Mercedes Benz!

Other sightings continued on an irregular basis. A silver Lamborghini Espada was a highlight one day; at the other end of the spectrum I had to ask a friend about the yellow coupe parked up near the school one day. This turned out to be a Ginetta G15, a pretty little glassfibre sports car. Lotus also figured largely in my repertoire and I came across Europas (one of which was local and reputedly owned by a chap who'd won the Pools) as well as the occasional Elan. At the bottom of the road in which I lived I occasionally glimpsed a Lancia Stratos in lime green. Whilst I had no idea how exotic this was back in the 1970s, I was taken by its purposeful shape: it had presence. By this time I was beginning to realise that I liked the oddball rather than the ordinary.

Then, in 1973, a new publication hit the news stands: *Classic Cars*. I think that one of my friends started buying it, and I followed suit. Here, at last, was something for the likes of us who weren't interested in cutting up cars to create something new or who were not solely enchanted by motor sport. This magazine was a revelation and must have fanned the latent flames that would erupt, in due course, into a lifetime's involvement with interesting vehicles.

If nothing else, *Classic Cars* broadened my automotive horizons. Seduced by lavish colour images of highly desirable (yet vaguely attainable) cars, I followed each issue with renewed interest. My particular memories are those of Rod Leach's Nostalgia advertisements in which there were always gorgeous cars that shrieked out to be bought. I recall, for instance, Lotus Type 95 Elites at a paltry £2,000 a time . . . Never mind the fact that this figure would have represented a couple of years' salary for someone who might be working in a bank at the time. I avidly read one correspondent's article on buying and running an Elite: he fronted a cream example that was, quite simply, drop-dead gorgeous. I slowly began to realise that it was the Lotus marque that appealed: the combination of beautiful styling and a shape that could not be confused with anything else made Colin Chapman's offerings something to be admired and coveted.

I was experiencing the pangs of falling in love . . .

*   *   *

In 1973 I began my driving lessons. To be honest, I couldn't wait. I was in the Sixth Form and it was The Done Thing. Not that I required persuading: only by going through the process would I be able to (hopefully) start off on that long road that would take me through decades of driving pleasure. I had no reservations or doubts about the Driving Test.

I would pass.

They were wonderful hours, those spent behind the wheel of a Mk1 Ford Escort, finding out about the intricacies of clutch control and reversing. My instructor was a lady with whom I got on famously and every other Saturday morning I could forsake the toil of a geography or history essay and find freedom and a kindred spirit on the road.

Ford's best-selling Escort must have provided the passport to a life of motoring for tens of thousands of baby-boomers

Looking back, the Escort was a splendid car upon which to have cut my teeth. Compact, comfortable and easy to drive, it had the bonus of an absolutely superb gearbox, the likes of which I have seldom encountered since. This was a real knife-through-butter gearchange and I can't for the life of me think why Ford subsequently played with it and diluted its appeal. Certainly, in the Reliant Scimitar 1600 which I acquired some years later, the Ford 'box was simply awful.

But I digress. I gradually built up my knowledge of the roads around Buckinghamshire and Bedfordshire and became acquainted with the Highway Code. There was little of note to report from those hours when I briefly became a Ford driver. Reversing around corners was aided by a strategically-placed paper clip in the rear screen rubber and I never did find out whether that was frowned upon by those examining one's driving skills in the test. Suffice it to say that I duly took my test and passed in 1974.

Then I wanted a car.

Like everything else in my life, nothing ever went according to plan. Leaving school at 18 with my A Levels, I eschewed university and went to work at the Midland Bank. Earning a salary was a bit of a novelty in 1974 and, being single, living at home and all the rest, I was quite well off – even if my monthly take-home pay amounted to about £85, which included overtime! A neighbour occasionally took me into Bedford and picked me up in his mustard coloured Ford Escort Mexico (which I believed at the time was no more than a basic Escort with some decals on its wings); otherwise, life was rather tedious. One highlight was an evening treasure hunt organised by the bank, in which I accompanied a colleague in his purple Triumph Spitfire: it was the first time, I think, I had been topless and that sensation has lived with me ever since. (This fellow subsequently drove the car to Poland with a friend where the Triumph proved little short of sensational, by all accounts).

Another colleague at the bank told me about a neighbour's son who sometimes rudely awakened him in the suburban peace of a Sunday morning when starting up his car. The car in question transpired to be a Lotus 7 and I duly met the anti-social scoundrel who took me for a ride one day. The sheer exuberance of speeding close to the ground in a flimsy orange *bolide* that cornered at silly speeds yet didn't slip off into the hedgerow was a completely new experience. Yes, it rattled and shook and made a lot of strange noises but I was hooked: Lotus really knew how to serve up the goods.

But there was more. Across the road from my bank was a rather trendy men's boutique that I frequented for ties. From time to time I saw a white Marcos slip into the parking slot near the emporium. I found out that it belonged to the shop's manager and in due course, obtained a ride in the low-slung product of Jem Marsh and Frank Costin's fertile brains. This was something else: knee-high to a grasshopper, it was the sort of car that had people craning their necks to ogle it. I was utterly captivated, even if the owner cautioned that care was needed to avoid the wooden-chassi'd vehicle bottoming out. One day, I thought, I'd like to own a car like this.

Finally, about two years into my banking career, came the great day: car ownership. From the first I'd decided that only a Lotus would do but my parents had other ideas. Parents always do—and I expect that I shall be the same when the time comes for my son and daughter to start driving. Anyhow, a Lotus was discounted on the basis of price, insurance and a hundred and one other, seemingly minor, things. In fact, it was to be another 15 or so years before I slipped behind that magical green and yellow logo.

In the interim I lapped up motoring books, particularly those that focussed on the less common British cars, of which there was no small number. A good many I have yet to clap eyes on, it has to be admitted: where are all the Deep Sandersons, GSMs and Fairthorpes hiding, I ask myself?

CHAPTER THREE

The French connection

1971 Simca 1000GLS

I'm a Francophile.

I make no bones about it and in fact, I rather relish the appellation. I've always thought that my interest in things French stemmed from a school trip that I took when I was 17 to the Loire Valley, even though I fell ill for several days following some jab that I'd had before my departure. It didn't put me off France one jot, though. This interest was fuelled by assembling and painting many French kits of figurines from the First Empire period; and watching French cinema and listening to French music. In my tastes, I was a bit different from everyone else I knew – which is possibly why I ended up with a Simca for my first car.

They say that one's first car is always something special and I suppose that in that statement there is an element of truth. If nothing else, having a car gives you undreamed-of freedom and the chance to drive wherever you wish. The only prohibiting factor is that of petrol – and the depth of your pocket.

Because we knew the chap with the gold Mercedes, getting on to the car ownership ladder was a straightforward process. I was looking at the bargain basement and in there we found the metallic gold Simca that was subsequently purchased, for I think, £695. He also had a bright yellow Ford Escort (funny how that car keeps turning up), but that was a £150 or so more expensive, so we passed on it. The Simca, a rather charmless, four door box, came with a three month warranty and several tins of red gunk that had to be added to the oil at regular intervals to validate the warranty.

(It was fortunate that it *was* under warranty, for a couple of weeks into ownership it went back to the garage to have an engine gasket replaced).

The GLS suffix on the car was always a mystery to me. I'd like to have supposed that it was an acronym for Goes Like Stink but, sadly, it wasn't. I believe it referred to the level of trim, which was one up on the LS. I never saw an LS, so I couldn't make a comparison. I did sight the occasional Simca 1100, which was equally ungainly, but the 1000 models remained surprisingly scarce.

Having the Simca meant that I could drive to work at last, which in turn allowed me to part company with buses and the interminable wait for the next one. It also meant that I had less money available since tax, petrol, insurance and all the other little things started to nibble away at my income. But having to abandon made-to-measure suits was a small price to pay for the joys of car ownership.

The Simca proved to be a reliable old thing, slow but sure, with a lengthy gearlever that I desperately wanted to shorten to make it look a bit sportier. However, this latter being fashioned from case-hardened steel made any reduction quite impossible.

Owning a Simca also made one stand a little apart from the likes of people who'd thrown their money into Ford or Leyland. Whilst these motoring giants fed the public's desire for accessories, a revenue source eagerly adopted by any self-respecting auto parts shop, for Simca owners there was absolutely nothing to buy. I envied friends who'd fitted a central console and who'd maybe added an instrument or two; I admired their fitted floormats; and I sighed over body accessories that only worked on other cars. Throwing furry rugs over the seats gave the Simca a cuddly, if hirsute appearance; and re-laying the carpet with off-cuts from the family's lounge floor covering added a certain chintz to the proceedings. But it was still a Simca underneath.

My time with the Simca made me realise that, despite my pedigree, I was not cut out to be a car mechanic. I'd bought the trusty Haynes manual early on, added a few oily fingerprints to it, and was always encouraged by the sight of the Simca 1000 Rallye that was pictured inside the cover. That was a *real* Simca although I never saw one burning up Mini Coopers around Buckinghamshire.

On one occasion the thermostat failed, so I duly purchased a replacement and set about dismantling the elbow in which the faulty unit resided. The three bolts were extracted with some difficulty, since I was relying on open spanners, not being in possession of a socket set. I managed to insert the new thermostat and replace the elbow, burring one of the bolts in the process. Then, when the engine began to overheat, I realised that I'd put the new part in upside down. And could I get the thermostat out again? That became a garage job, which was quickly followed by the purchase of my first set of socket spanners.

Overall, I did quite a few miles in the car and I recall 1977, if no other year, for that was when Tina Charles topped the charts with her effervescent, foot-tapping hit "I love to love". Not having a cassette player, I was reliant on good music coming out of the (very basic) Radiomobile that was fitted to the car. I remember that reception wasn't always too hot (I was going to find out in time how much worse it was in a Lotus with all that fibreglass!) but there was a tiny hole in the front of the set and within this sat a miniscule tuning screw. Well, I did dutifully twiddle but I don't think that it made any difference. To think that US cars had pre-set buttons two decades before . . . and there was I with a jeweller's screwdriver.

Long distance driving was occasionally undertaken: I drove the GLS up to Keele University one weekend, with my father on board, to visit my sister. It was winter and the car took ages to heat up because of the rear engine. It got there and back without difficulty and indeed, the car never broke down in the couple of years I owned it.

At some point during our relationship I found out that the Simca had developed a drink problem. More precisely, it was letting in water. I knew this because the rear carpets would be sodden to the touch after a rainstorm. However, finding the cause of the leak proved nigh on impossible so, in desperation, one weekend I stripped out all the interior and drove to work for several days in what approximated to a biscuit tin. It finally *did* rain again – and I was able to locate the source in the rear screen rubber. As the heated rear window element was also parting company, I very gingerly replaced it, too; and was delighted to be able to line up the new stick-on panel precisely on the first attempt, without damaging the delicate elements. Today, I imagine that any youngster would shrink from the very thought of trying to attach anything so flimsy and fragile.

I only ever had one hairy moment in the car that hailed from the land of garlic and Gauloises. It happened when I was driving into Bedford one frosty morning; the car executed a neat slide on the roundabout and finished up on the kerb at right angles to the traffic, much to the amusement of a group of schoolboys, who were awaiting a bus nearby. I sat there for a few seconds, waiting for a gap to continue on my route, when I espied out of the side window another car performing the same ballet step. In one of those surreal, slow-motion moments, the other car lost traction and began to slide straight towards me. I held my breath and the car stopped just as it touched my rubbing strip. The result was no more than a tiny dent in the chrome strip on the rear passenger's door, coupled with a huge expression of relief on the faces of both parties concerned.

The only other thing of note was that driving home one evening, the windscreen shattered. I've never been in a car since when this has happened and so the memory tends to remain. One moment clear vision, the next frosted glass. It's a strange sensation.

Arguably the most important thing about having the Simca was that it opened doors—literally—to other cars. I was totally shameless: spotting an interesting car for sale locally, I'd tootle over as a prospective buyer, just to get a drive in the vehicle in question. I tried Lotuses, a Ginetta, a Piper—even the ADD Nova to which I referred in an earlier chapter. I didn't buy any of these but I did begin to build up an appreciation of what exactly interested me. I also acquired a copy of Peter Filby's *Specialist Sports Cars*, a tome that opened up delight upon delight, for it focussed on low production, unusual British cars, the sort of thing that I realised I loved. Unbeknown to me, I'd later contribute articles to this chap's magazines.

Those years I spent with the Simca, although frustrating (since this was not exactly the type of transport to which I had aspired), did at least endow me with some useful No Claims Bonus and permitted me many hours of driving experience. I yearned for alternative in-car entertainment (it was the time when those massive eight-track cartridge players were all the rage) but that had to wait until my next purchase. And I think I carried three other people in the car on one occasion only, which just went to reinforce my conviction that cars with a longitude and latitude of seats were simply not for me.

As my finances were improving, and as the car was starting to develop those dreaded bubbles on its paintwork, so the time came to part company. The economy was suffering from oil price hikes by then (what's new? I hear you ask) so I gaily advertised a full tank of petrol for several hundred pounds – with a car thrown in. It took a while, but it did eventually sell. By then I'd lost interest in my French mistress – for I'd found a home-grown, sporty Oxfordshire model who was to be my bosom companion for nine years.

Cubism personified, the Simca 1000's box-like proportions were a photographer's worst nightmare. This is the only picture I ever took of the car and as such, a rare survivor

CHAPTER FOUR

Oxford blew

1974 MG Midget

Owning an MG immediately elevated me to the ranks of those Who Were Keen On Cars. Anything that has two seats (and possibly a soft-top) is, by definition, in certain circles at least, frippery and foolishness all rolled into one. That it's also fun too is usually overlooked.

Yes, I agree, subscribing to the two-seater brigade means just one thing: you're single (or at most, a couple) and without any further ties. A two-seater intimates that you enjoy life, driving and, if it's a soft-top, that you have a yen to commune with nature. Abingdon's little MG Midget was all of that and, because it was a rather run-of-the-mill little convertible, it was tolerated by those who might otherwise have been keen to cast the first metaphorical stone.

The car was sourced once again from my contact with the gold Mercedes, which guaranteed that it would be okay if anything untoward transpired; and, perhaps more importantly, it allowed me to persuade my parents that I was not going out on a limb and blindly buying something sporty. They obviously trusted me enough to go ahead with the car purchase, which was about £1,200. The previous owner, a lady, had become so pregnant that she couldn't fit behind the wheel, so her loss was my gain, if you'll excuse the paradoxical metaphor. The car was that glorious Citron Yellow colour, which would have been my first choice anyhow – and its shape, with those vestigial rear wings, endeared itself to me straightaway.

The year was 1978—and I was over the moon.

The pure and simple lines of the Midget were instantly recognisable on the road and Club members always waved at each other

Thirty years on, I still look back on MG ownership with a tear of nostalgia in my eye. It was, I suppose, the perfect car for me at the time: not complex, reliable, reasonably quick (but not excessively so)—and not exactly an insurance company's nightmare, either. That it was a convertible was a real bonus but then I'd already set my heart on topless motoring, having endured the extreme heat of the 1976 summer in my French tin box. My love affair with the MG was to last for nine years, partly because the car suited me so well, partly because I was shortly destined to go to university: and we all know that students have no money, far less access to sports cars. At least, that was the case back in the late 1970s. Interestingly, I still retain ties with this Leyland product in that both my current stablemates, to wit a Westfield X1 and a Mini Moke, rely on that trusty 1275cc block for their propulsion

I remember well the first jobs that had to be done on the car. Being thorough, I was keen to take the steel Rostyle wheels off because I knew that if wheel nuts were left *in situ* for undue lengths of time, they could seize on, making unplanned wheel changing something of a drama. The first one came off easily enough and I duly greased the studs before reassembly. The second was less straightforward and I ended up snapping off two of the bolts.

Fortunately, they were opposite each other so I was able to drive slowly to the local garage and let them sort it all out. Life's never easy, is it?

The other glaring deficiency in the car was that of in-car entertainment. There *had* been a radio, as evidenced by the messy, holed slab of wood that sat above the gear tunnel. That had to be re-covered with vinyl and I then sourced some pod speakers for mounting behind the seats, along with a tape player that was fitted to a slide-in, slide-out attachment, thereby leaving nothing inside the car that might tempt a thief. I also invested in a Crook-lok: remember those cumbersome sections of mild steel that terminated in red rubber curves that you looped around the clutch and the steering wheel? It was a sound investment, for I never lost the car.

Surf up, top down and the wind in your hair:
a car for the carefree connoisseur?

The car didn't require souping up nor did it require any addenda. I did fit a pair of headrests but that was about it: even the carpets, when I came to sell the car to a German enthusiast, were original. Along the way I got around to fitting a new hood, though; the doorskins were replaced and the car was partly resprayed, also.

In all, I think I went through a total of three windscreens. When the first one developed a crack I was, as always, down on my finances and I couldn't afford to call in AutoWindshields. Scanning the Exchange & Mart I came across a scrapyard in London that was breaking a Midget. A call revealed that the screen was available so off I went on the train, naively clutching a small bag of assorted spanners . . .

A few stops on the Tube later, and I was walking up the road to the yard. I think I fondly imagined that all the vehicles would be neatly laid out in rows, ready for dismantling. I was in for a shock: when I arrived, the MG was pointed out to me, perched up on top of two other cars. I quickly realised that my simple set of spanners was not going to be of much use.

However, someone there took pity on me and after a bit of an effort, they managed to unbolt the screen and its surround. I bought the lot (I think I paid about £15) and was then faced with getting it back home. Have you ever tried to carry a windscreen and surround through London? I must have been bonkers.

The assembly weighed a ton and it was all I could do to stagger few yards then rest before staggering some more. Somehow (I can't recall exactly how) I manhandled this lot through the Underground and on to a train before my father picked me up at Bedford station. It was duly fitted, much to my joy, and I considered the time and effort well spent. I don't think I'd want to repeat the experience today, somehow.

Another year of banking preceded a decision to attend college, and I took the MG to Lampeter, in Wales, where I studied English and French. I was one of about half a dozen students with a car and, needless to say, it was greatly admired, and often pressed into service on a Sunday night when someone would be stuck at a station 30 miles away. On one memorable evening a girl had been entertaining her sister for the weekend and she'd asked for a lift back to the station. Somehow she'd lost track of the time and all three of us (one squeezed into the back behind the seats) had a very rapid journey down to Carmarthen, where the sister, I'm glad to say, just caught her train in time.

Lampeter was also the start of many years of renting garages, something I still do today since I have not been fortunate enough to have found an affordable house with a triple garage block attached. Still, nothing's ever perfect, is it?

During ownership, one summer when I wasn't hand-painting the Rostyle wheels (!) we entertained a young French teacher who had come over with her pupils. Fabienne and I hit it off and we had a great time with the car. She invited me back to her parents' house in Rennes the following summer and I spent a few days there, delighted to be able to explore the area with herself and her sister, who also squeezed into the back of the car. Funny thing how the car always attracted trios – I suppose I should have gone out and bought a Matra Bagheera and had done with it.

Driving in France in a sports car brought home something to me, though. Simply everyone was fascinated by the MG. I've since come to realise that France is starved of interesting cars and so people will crane to look at something slightly out of the ordinary. The MG was sufficiently different to warrant attention and in years to come, I'd be venturing across the Briny in all manner of unusual cars that would have far more of an impact than the humble Midget.

Saturday evenings often meant attending the Rugby Club in Bedford, where there was usually a disco. I used to envy those smooth types leaving the building in a car with their roof down and a girl next to them. With the MG, I was able to join that select throng, although I only attempted the exercise once. Going from the heat of the dance floor to the chill of a summer's evening at midnight might have sounded romantic but the reality was a sore throat for a week. Topless night-time driving works fine in Acapulco but it was another matter entirely in Ampthill.

Whilst finishing my last year in banking I was actually working in Oxford, so was in my element with the car. I used to canoe there but now that college beckoned, I had to sell my canoe. This I sold to someone in the bank and I bravely offered to deliver it to her. It was freezing cold the night I chose and of course, the canoe had to be inserted into the passenger footwell as far as possible, with the rest sticking out over the seat and up into the air. With my left hand preventing the canoe from toppling over and falling on top of me, I somehow drove it through Oxford to its final destination.

Another time I was over in Portsmouth visiting a girlfriend. I'd espied a rather attractive cane bed head in a shop on the Saturday and so bought it, wedging it sideways into the car and into the recess behind the passenger seat. Of course, this necessitated talking the top down. Side vision was heavily impaired but I did drive back to Tunbridge Wells in this state, through two rainstorms—and picked up 'flu for my efforts. That wasn't the last time I'd carry odd loads in an unsuitable car, either.

Nine years with a car is a long time. In all, the MG only let me down twice: once, when the points closed up, I was left stranded at some traffic lights. On another occasion the water pump packed up on the way back from university, and I spent the afternoon in Cheltenham getting it sorted out. But that was the sum total, which says an awful lot in my book for the car's basic engineering.

My third year at college entailed a year abroad in France, and so I returned, this time to Corrèze, via St Malo. That 11 hour crossing was a real bind since I was always seasick. I worked in a school in Tulle where a German student teacher was also posted: he travelled around in a lime green Renault 4, with little checked curtains on the rear side windows, I seem to remember. Together, the cars made an eye-catching pair. The year was memorable for many things, not least the opportunities for travel that the MG afforded me. By this time I had developed an interest in number plates and was sporting ALW 2 on the car. This would later be changed to ATB 6.

For my year in France I deemed it expedient to fit protective meshes over the headlights. Well, French roads used to be bad . . .

When my car tax and insurance ran out that year and my Green Card expired, I had to attend to all of them. Actually, since the car was in France, the tax bit I skipped. Moreover, the local insurance agency couldn't find an MG Midget in its books: it did have a two door Allegro listed, though, so the car was insured as such . . .

Acquiring a French girlfriend along the way, I improved my language skills and was subsequently invited on holiday with the family, who drove down to Perpignan every year where they stayed on a big campsite. Suffice it to say there were no MGs around the area in 1982 and the car was in its element, basking in the hot weather. We toured chateaux and picturesque ports, lived on *paté* and *pain*, and even popped over to Spain one afternoon. Evenings were spent in a café overlooking the harbour in Collioure, where we played Travel Scrabble in French to the great interest of onlookers. Our idyllic month was cut short when we ventured to Nimes. Leaving the car to look for a hotel, we spent longer than anticipated and on our return we found that someone had broken into the MG. I lost my passport and two cameras (and more importantly, two films); sickeningly, it was the only time in nine years that I'd ever left anything in the car. One lives and learns, I suppose.

*   *   *

Back in the UK, I had a degree to finish. That last year was made a little more interesting by the fact that the MG began to exhibit signs of overheating. A friend diagnosed a silted up radiator so, armed with that trusty Haynes manual, I set about removing the radiator in order to have it flushed through. According to the manual, just six bolts hold it *in situ* and the whole affair is dismissed in a few lines. Well, reader, I can tell you that getting all the bolts undone was not the work of moments since some are virtually blind. However, I persevered and did finally get them all off, only to find that the radiator bottom hose, which is a neatly-twisted bit of tube in a very small space, just wouldn't shift an inch off the lower water pipe section. It was to all intents and purposes welded on. Enlisting the help of a muscle-bound rugby player, we did between ourselves eventually pull the hose off. It had taken a day in all, yet another salutary reminder to me that I was not cut out to be a motor mechanic.

My degree completed, I went off to Teacher Training College in the Midlands. It was an uneventful year, leavened only by getting to know a chap with a V12 E-type and seeing my first ever Fraser Nash. Wolverhampton and Dudley were barren ground for car spotters, even if the local dentist did drive a Pininfarina-styled Ferrari 308 GT4.

*   *   *

Life with an MG was thus never dull. I was pleased, looking back, that my car had been the RWA version, or round wheel arch, as they are known. These cars, made between 1971 and early 1975, looked the best of the bunch: prior to that the Midget's rear arch was flattened and, after the chrome bumper models, then came the awful US specification cars, with higher ride height and huge rubber bumpers. That killed any appeal that the Midget might have had in later years and the car's demise, in 1981, paved the way for the Mazda MX-5, which got everything right. I know—I've driven one.

From the driver's point of view, it's all been said: the MG handles predictably and doesn't do naughty things with its back axle like its cousin the Spitfire was prone to do. Yes, leaf suspension at the rear was pretty archaic by the mid 1970s and those leaves used to grate once they dried out, which proved tiresome. Otherwise, the car was well-behaved: it didn't drink fuel, its twin SU carburettors gave it a reasonable turn of acceleration and the gearshift was smooth, if it lacked a bit of damping and feel. It was cramped yet I did sleep in it once, on the docks in France at St Malo, when I missed a ferry back to the UK. It could also take a surprising amount of luggage, provided you relied on soft bags. I've never, ever bought cars for their boots, otherwise I'd have been hitched to a Volvo estate by now.

I fully entered into the spirit of MG ownership. I joined the Owners' Club, wrote poems and articles for the club magazine and saw myself in print. By then I was just starting a second career in teaching at a private Catholic girls' school in Tunbridge Wells. Whatever reservations I'd had about turning up in a yellow sports car were quashed when I saw an identical car in turquoise parked outside the school one day. Another teacher had a Midget too – so I was accepted.

A flat duly followed and then a hiatus. I began to write a motoring column in a local magazine, which allowed me to drive more modern cars. Time passed and I was content - but something was lacking. I needed variety, variety that would only come with the purchase of a second car.

Thus began my period of dual (and occasionally triple) car ownership.

Neat and compact, the MG was a joy – and it only broke down twice in nine years of ownership

CHAPTER FIVE

Essex toy

1972 Ginetta G15

I didn't have to think long and hard about what to buy. Some people, I know, like to own more than one example of a certain car but I could see little mileage (literally) in that. That wasn't for me: I was keen to get into fibreglass, since I was tiring of the constant attention that steel required in the fight against tinworm. Fibreglass held all the trump cards insofar as I was concerned: it didn't rust, it was light (so the car usually went quickly) and it generally resulted in a very pretty vehicle.

Thinking back to my A Level days, I knew what I wanted: a Ginetta. This was a pretty little car although at the time I had no conception of how big the range actually was. The G15 was neat and stylish; and the later (post 1971) models more attractive by dint of their faired-in front indicators and larger rear side windows. But I hadn't actually sighted one since I was 17, an indication of how rare they were, perhaps, so I joined the appropriate club and began to check the classified sections. It took a while: in those pre-Internet days, months could pass before something turned up. At last a car was discovered but it wasn't exactly local: it was in Manchester . . .

Undeterred, I took a train and went to view. The owner collected me from the station and took me for a spin and I was instantly captivated. The car wasn't immaculate by any stretch of the imagination and it had the 875cc engine as opposed to the more interesting 998cc lump. However, it had been uprated with a Kent cam so was quite entertaining. There were those all-to-become-too-familiar hairline cracks in the paintwork but on the plus side, it did have a Webasto sunroof. There was no fan (they weren't fitted as standard,

I recall) and that Hillman Imp alloy head was prone to warping if overheated, I knew from my homework. But such incidentals didn't dissuade me, for here was the next best thing to a Lotus Elan in my book.

I drove it back from Manchester with my heart in my mouth. Any new purchase is always an unknown quantity for the first few miles, after all. I began to worry when I saw fluid spattering on to the screen but that only turned out to be a loose pipe to the windscreen washer jet. We arrived back in Tunbridge Wells in one piece and the G15 was duly stored in a coach house next to my MG.

Life couldn't get any better, could it?

A convertible and a coupe gave me the best of both worlds, albeit double the garage bills

Having the Ginetta allowed me to compare the two cars, which was an exercise in itself. They were poles apart. I'd always considered the MG rather sporty but it came across as quite staid when compared to the G15. The latter was always raring to go and wasn't the sort of car that liked being driven slowly. Considering that its engine was only two-thirds the size of that in the Abingdon product, it went like the clappers. Cornering took on a whole new meaning with the G15: it went round bends as if glued to the tarmac. Ensconced behind that thick-rimmed wheel, my back barely supported by the short bucket seat, I was on a race track every time I twisted myself into the car's diminutive cockpit. Amazingly, a little over £5 would fill the tiny tank at that time and the only drawback to the car was that you'd lose it in a carpark because it was so small.

Having not one but two cars at school made me stand out somewhat. In the main it was accepted that I was a bit unusual but there was one teacher in particular who just could not understand why I should need two sportscars. With people like that it's all rather pointless trying to explain, I suppose. Rather more interesting was the rumour that started going around the school. The new English teacher was actually a millionaire (as evidenced by the two cars) and that he was merely teaching to kill a little time. Incredible, the status that multi-car ownership confers on one, isn't it?

I soon had a list of jobs that I wanted to carry out on the Ginetta but I was finding that owning two cars was not simply double the expense of having one—it was more. The steel wheels I really wanted to discard: I wanted some Cosmic alloys instead, since these looked just right on the G15. I also wished to install a fan and sort the seat pads out: their undersides were held together by copious application of duck tape which was constantly unpeeling with use. The carpets were a little scruffy—and the bodywork could really have done with a respray. One door was dropping slightly on its hinge, too, a fault common with fibreglass cars where there are pins that act as pivots, as I was later to discover with Lotus.

Mechanical access was enhanced by the flip-up bodywork. My 875cc aluminium engine was aided by a Kent cam and twin SU carburettors, although the 998cc version would have been even better

In the end, maintenance was restricted to a service (which revealed worn trunnions) and I managed to acquire a fifth (steel) wheel as a spare.

It was a lonely existence, too, driving a Ginetta. During my ownership I only ever saw one and on the day I spotted it, I was driving the MG! The Midget was much more sociable in that respect, since owners habitually acknowledged each other. However, like the MG, the G15 proved utterly reliable. A fuse blew on one occasion; the right angle drive failed and had to be replaced and one day I couldn't select reverse, which the local garage sorted out. That was it.

By the time I acquired the Ginetta I was also getting interested in car number plates. I suppose that it was down to the wordsmith in me: some people can't tolerate personal plates whilst others love them. I fell into the latter category.

Often likened to the Lotus Elan, the G15 gave its owner equal fun in the handling department but at a fraction of the cost of the Norwich product

Just after leaving the bank I was lucky enough to acquire ALW 2 from a dealer for the MG, as mentioned earlier on. This took a slice of my savings but I was happy to buy it, since I couldn't find my initials anywhere. A couple of years later the previous owner of the plate contacted me. He had lost this number through an insurance write-off and was anxious to get it back. I wasn't interested in selling but said that I'd consider parting with it if he could find me an ATB number of the same era. Amazingly, the DVLA helped him out on this and they dug out ATB 6, which had never been issued. A swap and cash adjustment ensued and thus began my love affair with cherished registrations.

Time passed, and I was kept busy teaching and writing—my spare time was occupied with articles on toys, old cars, restorations and modern car reviews. I was driving all manner of modern transport (with the occasional classic thrown in for good measure) when, one day, I did a road test on the new wedge-shaped Reliant Scimitar.

Suddenly I was catapulted out of the 1970s and into the late 1980s. In a word, I rather liked the Scimitar . . .

The pretty little G15 made use of a lot of proprietary parts but was none the worse for this "bin-raiding"

CHAPTER SIX

Pretty poly

1987 Scimitar 1600 & 1800ti

Two Scimitars?

Let me explain.

When I borrowed the 1600 for a road test for a local magazine, I came away smitten. I loved the shape. I loved the power that the 1600 brought. I also loved the hood, which was a masterpiece compared to that of the MG. The Abingdon product lacked a locating stud where the fabric meets the bodywork at the rear of the side glass and so contributes to the hood rising up its frame as it shrinks with age and wind buffeting. I loved the plastic bodywork, too. In short, I was ready for Tamworth's latest venture in the car world.

For car-spotters, the 1600 was easily identified by its plainer pattern wheels, double wipers and lack of side indicators

Billed as The Getaway Car, in Reliant brochures the Scimitar sat astride a huge compass, ready for action. It was blessed with electric windows and mirrors (something I'd never experienced before) and it was wedge-shaped, which was very much in vogue in the mid-eighties. Reliant was still a joke for many drivers, of course, because it still peddled three-wheelers and was famous for those ubiquitous light blue invalid cars. Princess Ann had bestowed a certain cachet upon the company, though, through her endorsement the estate-like SE4a. With the SS1 series, however, Reliant was breaking new ground—and moulds.

The dramatic shape was just right for the time, aping as it did the likes of the TVR 350 and the Lotus 500 range. Curves were out—sharp edges and flat surfaces were the order of the day. I hankered after an example soon after the road test and thus had to sell both the MG (which went to Germany in the end) and the G15 (I can't recall the buyer of that one). Even then I lacked the balance to buy the 1600: to be exact, £2,000. Fortunately, that saviour of Young Men with Car Problems came to my rescue: my mother. I duly located a white example near Hastings and took my mother for a drive, simply to impress upon her that the car had my name written all over it. I drove the car home, as happy as that fellow named Larry.

Sleek and purposeful, the 1600 certainly looked the business although it wasn't particularly rapid with the Ford engine

The SS1 1600 was great fun but only for a short period of time. Whilst I liked the layout and pretty nearly everything about the car, its fifth gear didn't endear itself to me too much. This involved a really awkward movement of the gearstick: somehow, Ford (or Reliant) had got it all wrong. And then, to cap it all, my local dealership took into stock a brand new white SS1—but with Nissan Sylvia turbo power. Coupled with fuel injection, here was something quite different from the cooking 1600: as the Sales Manager said to me, "it goes like s— off a shovel." It was no use—I had to lay hands on the turbo'd version.

I was friendly with the garage and they kindly offered to take in the 1600 for what I had paid for it against the new 1800ti. A loan later and the car was mine: it had cost a little over £11,000, by far the most expensive car I'd ever owned. But a change of job and better prospects meant that I could swallow the pill; and since I habitually worked through my summer holidays, I consoled myself and justified the purchase. Easy when you try, isn't it?

Life with a 1987 1800ti was just fine – and that is an understatement. The car was extremely responsive, thanks to that turbo, and with a lovely Japanese gearbox it was light years away from the Ford-sourced car. Reliant also produced a 1300cc model but to be honest, none of the SS1 cars was a big seller. People didn't like the styling or they fought shy of the badge: whatever, I seldom saw one on the roads thereafter.

By this time I had met my wife-to-be, who lived at the other end of the country, near Bath. A fair bit of motorway commuting became the order of the day and whilst the SS1 was perfectly adequate for this, I used to also try and borrow a car for the weekend to cut down on its annual miles. This was easy since I was still writing a motoring column. Thus I'd turn up in a BMW or a Suzuki Jeep or whatever I could lay my hands on; I think Helen's neighbours believed that I was a second-hand car salesman.

Despite its performance, the 1800ti version was destined to become an uncommon sight on British roads

Faults? The SS1 had none, save that after any long journey, or when the engine was really hot, you had to let the engine idle and turbo cool down before switching off. Failure to observe this would result in the car depositing embarrassing quantities of water. Also, the front fog lamps, which were hardly ever used, were sited very low and used to pick up chips and stones, as well as water, which meant that the metal casing rims would start to corrode. I had to resort to filling the gaps with thick grease but it never really solved the problem. Oil had to be changed religiously every 3,000 miles, too: I took out an extended warranty with the car, which was just as well, for the turbo failed at 30,000 miles, which apparently was quite normal, despite its being looked after. That bill was over £1,000 but I was covered.

Other niggles were the seats, which were lovely when new. Mine had the grey Alcantara finish and not the leather but keeping them clean-looking was a nightmare. I used chalk dust to try and get the colour back but the seats just got darker and darker with the passage of time (and, dare I say it, my backside). There was also an intermittent wiring problem under the bonnet: sometimes the car wouldn't start and so I had to jiggle the loom slightly to make the contact. But these were minor nuisances compared to the sheer pleasure of cruising around on a hot day with the tape-player turned up: and all that power under one's right foot was something to be savoured.

The only mishap during my ownership occurred on the beach front at Hastings. I'd parked the car in a line of sundry vehicles and motorcycles and when I returned to Woozle, I was horrified to see that a motorbike had toppled over in the gusty conditions and had come to rest on the boot. The fibreglass was dented and cracked and, predictably, there was no-one around to claim responsibility. My local bodyshop quickly repaired the mess and from that day forward, I've never parked next to a motorcycle again.

About this time I decided to sell ATB 6 to help finance the 1800ti. I duly found a buyer and then immediately decided that the car was rather bare without the distinctive registration. Looking around I chanced on WOO 40. Why this plate? Well, being a writer, I have a weakness for Olde Englishe and this word appealed. In addition, it looked like I might be marrying this lady in Bath—so the plate would be ideal for a wedding car. This turned out to be true and the car was cleaned up so as to be spick and span on the Big Day: in fact, there was hardly a mark on her. I was later to discover (in fact, only after I'd parted with the car) that the SS1 relied on polypropylene for its bodywork: I'm not aware of any other car that used this material at the time and indeed, whether any actually has employed it since. All I can say is that the material wears amazingly well and the car's bodywork looked like new when she was sold.

But I'm getting ahead of myself a little here. Before weddings and honeymoons and things of that nature, another love entered into my life. This was only made possible by moving from my flat in Tunbridge Wells to a small house near Maidstone. My financial advisor (another friend) arranged my mortgage so that I had some spare cash as an offset. Trouble was, spare cash and a liking for cars make for ill-assorted bedfellows and the two were, in fact, mutually exclusive . . .

So, if you want to blame someone for the next chapter, blame my financial advisor.

Woozle, as she was dubbed, was always at home in hot climes: the hotter, the better.
She took us to France on several occasions

CHAPTER SEVEN

Ally pally and a seventh heaven

1927 Austin Seven Super Accessories

1930 Austin Seven Ulster Replica replica

1956 Austin Seven Hamblin Cadet

I can see the question forming on your lips, dear reader.

Why on earth would someone who's totally happy with his lot be looking at acquiring *another* car?

The reason here, I well recall, lies buried in an old copy of *Thoroughbred and Sports Cars* which, along with the *Sunday Times*, filled in the gaps between my trips to Bath. (I was teaching in a public school at this time and that meant Saturdays were often taken up, so trips down the M25 and M4 were not regular occurrences).

The article in question was postulating the availability of classic cars and what constituted a good starter classic. Having a modern car (however much fun it was) did mean that I was out of touch with the old car scene, which irked me a little. The magazine looked at three possible starters; however, I can only remember the Triumph Herald and the Austin 7 saloon that featured. There was something about the Austin that intrigued me. I can't rightly say what it was now, but something tugged a string: perhaps it was the concept, hitherto undreamed of, let alone attempted, of pre-war motoring. I had visions of myself, pottering Toad-like, around Kent's leafy lanes and being at one with nature in my checked flat cap. My Austin 7 phase was about to begin.

As usual, I started to do my research and attended the local Austin 7 meetings. I was the youngster there but I quickly got used to the older generation's ways that would see, for example, sage owners pass around a cloth bag which contained a part from a 7: the object was to feel the bag and declare what it was. Some members just took their knitting along. I was lucky enough at one meeting to persuade a chap to allow me to drive his rather tired Chummy. I immediately formed a bond with the long-deceased Herbert Austin and his tiny brainchild. I began to read the 750 Club magazines more closely and then it dawned on me that the Ruby and Chummy and Top Hat vehicles of this world were not what I wanted. No, they were far too staid: I was after something more sporty, something that would stand out from the crowd (yet again). I guess that by now you can see where I was heading: Special ownership beckoned. The subsequent purchase of that A7 bible, namely *Austin Seven Specials* by Bill Williams, sealed my fate.

I could never take myself totally seriously in an A7 – hence the
radiator mascot!

Finding an Austin 7 Special took a little while, though. The club magazine occasionally had one for sale but generally they were rather ugly-looking to my way of thinking. That was the trouble with the Special: rule books were abandoned as time or money (or both) ultimately dictated the end design. There were some really pretty cars about, mind you, such as the Ulster Replica and the Nippy but these were not true Specials. It was thanks to an anonymous small ad in the good old *Exchange & Mart* that I ended up in Bournemouth one day to see a boutique owner who had an Austin 7 for sale for £2,500, one which boasted a homemade body. The chap knew nothing about the car save that it had been on a farm in Texas, taken overseas by some Brit years before. He'd somehow inherited it (complete with faded CHT 62 number plates) but there was no logbook. The car was a short wheelbase version and didn't run; it was also very tatty inside and had no hood. Against that was the fact that it was endowed with beautiful flared front wings and tidy rear cycle wings: it looked for all the world like a miniature Morgan, a car whose aesthetic beauty none could deny. It was the first time that I'd ever contemplated buying a car that I couldn't actually test drive; it was also really too small for me since I was five foot eleven and, ideally, suited to the later, longer wheelbase Austins.

But it was pretty . . .

Very pretty.

Clothed in aluminium, the Super Accessories Special was a world away from the concept of motoring for the masses that Herbert Austin had envisaged in the 1920s

Around the same time, again in the *Exchange & Mart* and this time within the Cherished Numbers section, I spotted arguably the most interesting number plate of all time. For some time I'd toyed with the desire of owning one particular number plate, one I had seen in a secondhand book on the subject in Foyles' motoring section a few years back. This kind of hankering is often just a pipedream where number plates are concerned: cars get scrapped or owners pass on their plates to offspring—or they are offered at silly prices if ever they do come on to the market.

The plate in question, 20 FUS, was actually shown on a wedding car with the (then) owners, Jackie Trent and Tony Hatch, crouched in front of it. Unless you know a little about the musical duo, then the significance of this number is lost on you. Jackie Trent was well-known for her best-selling "Where are you now my love?" track whilst Tony Hatch was a prolific music composer and arranger—to him we owe themes such as "Crossroads" and "Neighbours." They married (but later divorced!) and on their wedding day they released a lesser-known single, "The two of us." Hence the significance of the number plate which one of the dealers now had for sale.

I was in quandary: I liked the 7 but the plate was a one-in-a-million opportunity. I recall telephoning Helen to ask her opinion, which went something like "You'll have to make the choice."

So I did.

The number plate was acquired and since I had no car for it, it was put on a friend's Ford Sierra. A colleague in the motor trade had a low loader and a little later the strange Austin 7 came back to live in Kent.

I subsequently discovered that I'd bought a Super Accessories car, quite a rare beast, with fewer than 20 known to the club.

The Super Accessories originated, somewhat surprisingly, from the cosy London suburb of Bromley all those years ago, where a modest workshop supplied the wants of the hard-up motorist with sporty pretensions

Thus began the task of getting the Austin through the MOT. I'd never been down the road of partial restoration before and the Austin was a good introduction to the subject. It quickly became apparent that I'd need all the instruments refurbished; a new dashboard would need to be made; the engine would need fettling; new seats and a hood and carpet would have to be sourced; and the wheels and tyres needed looking at. Fortunately, the bodywork was in good shape although the bright red hue was too strident for the age of the car.

Another colleague of mine, who'd been employed at the Reliant dealership, had recently gone solo to restore Morris Minors and he agreed to do the work, thereby leaving me free to track down all the sundry bits and pieces.

*   *   *

To be fully understood, the Super Accessories has to be viewed in the context of its era, and so it's worth a few words of explanation, I feel. The aftermath of the Second World War saw a Britain getting back on its feet, after what had been a debilitating six years. Rationing still affected many walks of life and indeed was to linger on into the 'fifties for some products. And for the young at heart but impecunious of pocket, motoring was not exactly at its apogee, the industry only just beginning to think in terms of production that wasn't solely directed towards the war effort. Just about anything mechanical was in short supply—as was the power to make it go. Sports cars were very much the preserve of the well-heeled and it would have been a lucky young chap indeed who had access to something racy such as an MG, a Morgan or a Singer.

But in the face of adversity ingenuity, as ever, triumphed. If showroom cars were in short supply and priced in extra-terrestrial terms, there were plenty of old Fords and Austin 7s still about. A goodly number would have weathered the war years tucked away in garages, permitted the occasional sortie if petrol coupons and funds permitted. Imagine a car in your garage and you being unable to drive it . . .

Body stripped, the hitherto red car is prepared for a re-spray in dark blue

So these venerable old workhorses, which had earlier brought motoring within the reach of millions, were once more dusted off and gradually returned to the King's highway. And so our penniless young bloods began to take a second look at these relics of the twenties and thirties. Admittedly, your bog-standard Ruby or Chummy wouldn't have done much for your street credibility in the late 1940s—but then the term hadn't been invented, so perhaps it didn't matter that much. No, the Ford and Austin were just crying out for some modifying . . .

Enter the Special.

This type of car was to become for many the worthy alternative to those flashy low-slung convertibles that were occasionally glimpsed speeding down twilight country roads, usually occupied by some rake and a pretty female companion, scarves a-curling in the breeze. Whilst it would be hard to identify exactly when the Special came of age, what *is* certain is that the concept and philosophy had great appeal to more than a few. An old Ford or Austin could be had for a song—and by the mid-fifties, there were plenty to choose from. After all, the earliest were three decades old by then.

In much the same way as motor racing was once a sport for the enthusiast with little cash but some mechanical knowledge, so it was with the construction of Specials. Just how often and how competitively one raced at club level would have been dictated by funds—and the Special constructor was faced with the very same set of parameters. From those early pioneers who "did it themselves the hard way" there followed waves of interest, so much so that some enterprising manufacturers sprang up to cater for the would-be car builder and thus make available useful engine ancillaries or bodywork and mechanical parts. The names of Speedex, Cambridge Engineering, Dante and Super Accessories were just four such companies: and it was this latter company that I was to focus on.

In 1956 one Les Montgomery, aged 36, shaped a wooden frame which was intended for fitting to an Austin 7 chassis. Using his cousin's car as a guide, this design exercise was loosely reminiscent of the Vale Special of 1934/35 and a Ford/Morgan three wheeler. The moment of truth came later in the year when he acquired an Austin 7 van: he fitted the ash framework and clothed it aluminium panels. From these humble beginnings was born the Super Accessories.

True to the spirit of those golden years, things were done in alarmingly simple fashion. The bodies were created from a single sheet of 20 gauge aluminium, approximately 8 x 4 ft in size, and the template, a section of linoleum(!), served throughout the car's six year production life. Bonnet and spare wheel panels were cut from another sheet of the material. Bonnets on surviving Super Accessories are rarely the same: the company, cognisant of the fact that the height of radiators on A7s varied, could supply a rough shape (in two pieces) for the buyer to trim and modify as desired. The dictates of pedal room and engine size, together with the possibility of a centrally-hinging bonnet, were all factors to be considered by the amateur builder.

The bodyshell proper tipped the scales at just 35lbs for the shorter wheelbase (6'3") Austin, with the later models, the 6'9" cars, needing a 40lb shell. As work got underway, two shells could be manufactured each week. The price of this bespoke engineering? Just £5. And if you couldn't make it to the workshop in Bromley, then it could be delivered by passenger train to anywhere within the UK for an extra 50s (or £2.50).

But the shell and frame were just the beginning. Whilst the cars were not intended for track use (their final weight was a limiting factor), the buyer would still have to modify a chassis. Those really into the Special philosophy boxed in the 7 chassis for extra strength and then set about lowering the suspension. A Bowdenex set-up was most desirable and naturally coil over spring shockers were looked upon with favour. A lowered and raked steering column was required; the windscreen and frame could be ordered for 19s 6d and this included "Liftadot" fasteners in place, ready for a hood. The hood itself, with a simple frame which could be separated and stowed (just) behind the seats, worked out at just a few pounds. And then came the cycle wings, seat cushions and front headlight stays . . . The list, rather like Topsy, could grow but the enthusiast could budget accordingly—or make do and modify. Instruments, engine, brake parts and the like could all be sourced from the donor A7. However, those opting for something quick would have to jettison the brakes—after all, the cable variety were only just able to stop an A7 in normal guise. Hydraulics were the ultimate for such a special.

Of course, having gone to all the trouble of sourcing an A7, discarding the bodywork, buying and modifying and attaching a new frame and body and decking out the car with the desirable options (yes, an outside exhaust was the order of the day, very much *à la* Lotus 7), it would have been a crying shame not to have completed the exercise and gone to town on the engine. The beauty of Herbert Austin's little 747cc lump was that it could be tweaked and teased and the bhp upped. In its early days it gasped out 10bhp (by 1926 this had increased to a puny 24bhp), whilst supercharging could add a further 9bhp. But as superchargers were not within most people's budget, so fiddling and tuning came to be the avenues exploited.

A Supaloy head coupled to a Dante manifold and a downdraught Zenith gave a modest increase in bhp to the standard tiny output

A desirable special of the era would have boasted the company's aluminium Supaloy head which, when fitted, gave a 6.5 compression ratio; a large capacity alloy sump and four branch banana manifold completed the set-up. Carburettors were to choice: Zenith were popular, the downdraught being the one to go for, but A7s did accept SUs also. As the catalogue of the time reveals, fitting a Supaloy head "will even make your old saloon go like a Sputnik!" Where could you find such claims today? In actual fact the cylinder head was designed by Graham Broadley; his cousin, Eric, is best remembered for his work on the Lola racing cars. Super Accessories offered plenty of desirable gubbins of this nature and would re-bore old blocks, oversize your inlet valves and carry out the myriad little jobs that would make your Special something more than just a Chummy in fancy dress.

Bringing in his father to help in the business, Les found that demand was soon outstripping supply and after just three months, Montgomery senior gave up his furniture trade job and concentrated full time on his son's enterprise. Indeed, such was the demand for this winning formula that the bodywork was eventually farmed out to local craftsmen, leaving the father and son free to explore other Special possibilities and to reinforce the stock of spares. Final work on the shells was done in the Bromley workshops before collection or despatch.

The arrival of Brian Montgomery (Les's son) in 1959 brought fresh impetus to the company and he took over the administration side.

As the business became better known and its reputation grew, so Les and his father looked for ways to expand. A deal with Keith Bowden from Devon allowed the Bromley company to sell on independent front suspension units designed by Keith. A little later Les joined forces with Hamblin, a company in Dorset selling fibreglass shells, also designed to accept Austin 7 mechanicals. This pretty little convertible had the looks of a single seat racer of the era – as you'll find out in due course.

Keen to capitalise on whatever the public whim, Les realised that Austin 7s were only part of the equation, so he began to experiment with the idea of a body that would accept Ford E93A parts: the 1172cc engine was, in its turn, destined to become popular with Specials builders. Thus the Super Two entered the arena and the body/chassis package retailed at £9. The larger body was built on a 2" box section chassis. More and more design work followed: the sumps and cylinder heads were to end up being cast by a concern in Coventry whilst Super Accessories also developed a close-ratio gearbox, successfully used in competition by Jack French, a noted Austin 7 authority. In addition, close ratio gears were developed for the Ford sidevalve Special.

But, like so many other motoring phases, the mania for Specials peaked and then dwindled. One of the main reasons was the availability of more modern cars with sporting pretensions which were much more advanced in terms of comfort and mechanical engineering: by 1962 the Fairthorpe, the Midget and Frogeye Sprite were on the scene, and a new contender was taking the world by storm: the Mini. Records from the Bromley company are scant but it is reckoned that altogether some 220 Super Accessories bodies were manufactured over the six year period.

Interior was basic, relying on padded squabs, a wooden dash and the odd salvaged instrument. Glovebox was just that – big enough for a pair of driving gloves and nothing else

My car had probably started life as a 6'3" wheelbase Chummy and was unknown to the 750 Club: it thus became the 17th survivor. She was overhauled during the next year and refurbished where necessary. In many ways the car was an excellent example of what a Special, and particularly a Super Accessories, was all about. Bristling with all the goodies (Bowdenex suspension, Supaloy head, Dante manifold, downdraught Zenith and coil over shocks all round), this Super Accessories looked the part. She retained her six volt electrics, which were a mixed blessing: originality counts for much, of course, but practicality meant that unless the battery was fully charged, after a couple of churns on the starter, the thing would be flat. Consequently, the starting handle was a boon. Yet another drawback to "half a battery" was nocturnal travelling: whereas decades ago one could bravely go down minor (and even major) roads with just sidelights ablaze, in 1990 this was not practical. And try as the dynamo might, ten minutes' worth of headlights would begin to sap those precious volts. But after being re-upholstered (very basically) and equipped with a new dash and hood, she was a lovely looking vehicle.

The last owner had obviously spent money on the car, so complete was the specification. True, the brakes were a mixture (hydraulic front with cable rears): with no compensator, it made slowing down an interesting practice. Although synchromesh was weak on all gears, the simple "in or out" clutch with half an inch of play was soon learned, and double de-clutching became routine. The horrifying slop in the steering was also overcome: all A7s have it apparently! Even the bugbear of the short chassis I lived with. But for readers around six foot, these older Austin 7s are best avoided if you want to get your legs into the footwell at all.

Off-road, the Special proved equally entertaining, as Helen found out

It's a quixotic thing, but half the enjoyment in doing up old cars is finding the parts. A car show/ autojumble yielded an elusive ammeter that was encased within a dredger dashboard (!) whilst a lot of the bread and butter bits were sourced from A7 parts people. One particular Yorkshire enterprise that became well-known to me dealt only in cash: you posted banknotes to cover the cost of the items, plus a guess at postage, and received some days later the requisite parts, plus change . . .

Perusing the club magazine during this period, I came across another interesting vehicle, to wit and unfinished Ulster Replica (or rather, a replica of that car). It sported that distinctive alloy bodywork and was fitted with a machine-turned dash, engine, gearbox and all the running gear but required wiring, the interior finishing and sundry other stuff. It was cheap (around £1,700); it was very attractive; and to my way of thinking, a gorgeous-looking car, because the boat-tailed Ulster really epitomises the racy side of the Austin 7 equation.

One that I didn't make earlier: the replica Ulster would have made a stunning Special, but sadly funds ran out

Often these cars end up on race tracks or take part in hill climbs, but they are quite practical for road use, too

Now, to be honest, I didn't need another Austin 7 project. What I needed was a rich wife who owned a garage, perhaps, but not another car. However, the opportunity was too good to miss and since my friend had plenty of storage space at his workshops, this solved the garaging problem. I spent some time working on the car but did little to it although I had the dials refurbished and got in the queue for a new radiator surround (the Ulster came with a fibreglass substitute). There was only one chap who supplied the Austin 7 club with this item, and so patience was a virtue when it came to his production line.

At this point things began to get really complicated.

*　　*　　*

The farmer with whom I'd originally lodged the Super Accessories (his son attended the school at which I taught and the father, usefully, had an interest in old cars) also ran an auction from time to time. Some were collective sales, others featured cars. He mentioned casually one day that he had a rather unusual car in one of his barns for the coming auction . . . Well, I had to have a look, didn't I?

The Austin Nash Metropolitan I'd not seen since I was tiny and even then, they were a scarce commodity. The farmer had been offered a 1961 turquoise and white convertible for auction. The story ran that the owners had been killed in a car crash (not in this car, I hasten to add) and that the car formed part of the estate that was being liquidated for a surviving child. It was a sad tale and the car itself was in a sadder state. Essentially complete insofar as I was aware, the car had suffered from extensive rot and although it was holed in places and rusty just about everywhere else, the structure was sound overall. Predictably the engine bay was neglected but the interior wasn't too bad at all, with the distinctive black and white houndstooth check seat coverings untorn. The Nash radio was there, too. It being a convertible, the car immediately caught my fancy and because it looked like an overgrown 1960s bumper car, straight out of the fairground, I was seduced.

The auction I duly attended, certain that I was going to win the car because, quite simply, no-one else had seen it and spent hours with it like I had. You can imagine my disappointment when I reached my bidding limit and someone else was prepared to go higher. I subsequently met the new owner, who lived in the Medway towns, and we exchanged contact details since I was keen to see this car back on the road one day.

In retrospect, with three cars already, a fourth might have tipped the balance and sent me down the road to insanity. At least that's what Helen thought, although she never said as much. But collectors of anything have to be a bit eccentric—don't they?

So, back to the Austins. The Super Acc (as they were referred to) was coming along well. The radiator surround and headlight bar had been re-chromed; the dash was in place and the instruments were back. A swap with a chap had seen me part with the original battered brass headlamps and acquire a lovely lever action filler cap assembly that was simply perfect for the car. The wipers worked (just) and the old willow-wand-in-porridge gear shift had been cut and transformed into a remote change, which was much slicker and more in keeping with the car's character. The seat back transpired to be a section cut out of a Stop: Children Crossing sign (!), and so was retained for historical reasons.

The car was duly resprayed Rover Admiralty Blue, which set the chrome off well. A climbing toad mascot topped off the bakelite radiator cap: all it needed was a hood and we were away.

The trimmer I used was in Hastings so I duly drove the car down one day, marvelling at the wobbly steering that required constant correction. They all do it, I was told—so one just got used to it. About 20 miles into the drive the engine coughed, spluttered and died. The 6 volt starter couldn't resurrect the old girl, either. Looking around the engine bay all that I could see that was guilty was the little glass petrol bowl that preceded the carburettor. This was murky with sediment, indicating dirty petrol. The AA man duly appeared and sorted it out but the problem recurred on the return trip, again around the 20 mile mark. Subsequent chats with the Morris garage revealed that the petrol tank hadn't been removed from the car. That was the next job.

Christobel, as she came to be known, (for Swansea had magnanimously allowed the registration to stand, despite the flimsiest of evidence), then gave Helen and I many miles of eventful motoring. She usually received a lot of attention and drives in her were always slightly uncertain affairs. For starters, there was the starter. As mentioned, lights mysteriously dimmed at night-time as the battery's power succumbed to the unwelcome extra wattage demands placed on it; tyres squealed on roundabouts taken at anything over 20 miles an hour;

and you felt every jolt despite a fairly sophisticated Bowdenex suspension set-up. The needle on the speedometer gauge gave you an indication of how fast you were travelling (you took the high and low readings and settled on a happy medium), whilst at anything over 45mph the car felt inherently unsafe.

(Actually, in retrospect, it probably was).

Maintenance on the move was standard practice with Christobel

We attended car shows and actually won a second prize on one occasion; it was probably down to the fact that our car was new on the scene, a scene that did rather attract the same old members and the same old cars at the same old events, year after year. We even did a bit of a gymkhana in a field once, which brought home to my wife that Austin 7 driving wasn't really her thing at all. A pity really, since she fitted it perfectly. I also had the honour of writing up the restoration for *Popular Classics* magazine, in which I featured at (relative) speed.

At anything over 30mph in Christobel you took your life into your hands . . .

Some months later the head gasket blew and this necessitated work on the block and an impressively large bill. The novelty of the Austin 7 began to wear off after that particular episode. Also, with the money having been spent on the restoration, I couldn't proceed with the Ulster that was waiting, wingless, in the wings. The time had come to rationalise my life again.

What really caused the shake-out in the end was a call from the owner of the Metropolitan: he'd found a restored car so had decided to sell the Berkshire Green and white example that I had tried so hard to win at auction. Surprise,

surprise, he was looking for about the same money that he'd paid for it. Mets, as they are known in club circles, were thin on the ground at the best of times and this was a soft top into the bargain. So, to cut a long story short, I managed to offload the Ulster to another enthusiast and spent the money on the Metropolitan.

The right weather helped on The Big Day: here's the belle in all her glory
(Helen, that is, not the car . . .)

Around this time (1992 to be exact) I got married to Helen, since we were getting tired of travelling up and down the M4 on an irregular basis. Woozle (as the Scimitar was known because of her number plate) was the (topless) bridal car used after the reception and was suitably adorned (without my knowledge) with numerous balloons and tin cans.

After the reception we set off with a small bouquet to place on a gravestone en route to the supper and duly stopped at the cemetery where Helen laid the posy. She also temporarily put the bridal floral decoration on the car's bootlid whilst performing this act. Forgetting the flowers were there, we drove off only to recall our error some miles later . . . A U turn and an anxious quarter of an hour ensued before we sighted the flowers at the roadside. Not the best start to married bliss, perhaps. Woozle then took us on honeymoon to northern France where it rained a lot (well, it *was* the Easter holiday break). However, we didn't complain, and filled the car with essentials on the way back, including a five piece Le Creuset saucepan set which Helen had to nurse all the way home. As I said earlier on, I never was one for practical cars.

Tiring of the Austin 7 Super Acc, I put her up for sale to recoup some of my investment. I say "some" since I never have set out to make money on cars: I love them too much for that. A buyer was located (funnily enough, another German) and he came over to Harwich on the ferry, drove the car around the dock and then paid up. It's probably the only Super Acc in the Fatherland and I hope that he enjoyed it.

I was sad to see Christobel go but something else had appeared on the horizon, in Norfolk to be exact.

Having enjoyed aluminium, I was ready for fibreglass and the car in question, a Hamblin Cadet, was a sporty-looking cigar shape, which also sat on Austin 7 running gear. This came with cycle wings, a 12 volt battery (no more starting problems!), no windscreen, an interior that was nicely trimmed and a gearshift already converted to the remote variety. In fact the owner had done a lot of work to the car, which was a real rarity: like the Super Acc, the bodywork could be specified to fit both long and short chassis Austin 7 models and, I recall, could even be adapted for Ford running gear. The body itself had plenty of holes in it (drilled, as opposed to rust) but the car did go—although the owner confessed that the cooling system wasn't working quite right. This didn't worry me, having been through the mill with the Super Acc: I felt that I knew what I was in for and that I could find the necessary people to put matters right.

A deal was struck and the car was brought back to Kent and taken to my local father and son garage, Frank and Paul Dadson, a place that specialised in older cars. The pair set to work on the Cadet and soon had the cooling system re-jigged so that the engine stopped overheating. Meanwhile, I was left with the tough choice of screen: either those cute (but impractical) flyscreens or something approaching the original. By an amazing chance I located another Cadet over in East Kent and went to see it and chat to its owner. At least I then had an idea of what the screen was like. To be honest, I held out little hope of finding a proper screen but a chance small ad in the Austin 7 magazine yielded a reply. This chap in Worcestershire had a spare screen but he didn't know what it was off: did I have anything to swap? From the description and dimensions it seemed like it might fit the Cadet and for my part, I had an alloy Austin 7 head that was surplus to requirements. We swapped and I awaited impatiently the screen, which my wife brought down to Kent after a visit to her parents who lived in Malvern. I immediately tried it on the bodywork but it sat proud; but then, tilting it, you can imagine my joy as the side strakes sat snugly against the car's curves and the rounded base of the screen nestled on to the fibreglass.

Success!

A 12 volt battery and, at length, the right windscreen, helped make the Hamblin a delight to drive

Looking back, this was just another example of the luck that I've had with my cars down the years. I've read all the horror stories of buying a classic (and even written a book about the subject) but I've never bought a pig in a poke. Someone up there (or perhaps, more precisely, under the car) has watched over me.

The Cadet, rather like the Super Acc, came without paperwork but once it was working satisfactorily it was then a case of getting it registered for the MOT. At the time Swansea was putting Scottish number plates on older cars that couldn't provide history: these are easily identified at car shows and the like because they invariably contained the letter S. I wasn't keen on the idea since some car enthusiasts want originality and nothing less. As luck would have it, a friend of the garage had in his possession a buff log book without a car and the six digit number thereon suited the car perfectly. I think £50 changed hands and I was then left to square things with the DVLA.

Hamblin interior was better finished than those of my previous Austins. Note the indicator knob mounted on the transmission tunnel, just behind the remote gearchange

Life with the Cadet went without a hiccough. The car had been well built and my only bugbear was that the body really needed to have its holes filled in (it had acquired a few more by this time, as lights had been re-sited) and the whole thing resprayed. Sadly, this never happened. The large Austin 7 steering wheel had to go: I found a neat, small diameter, well-dished wooden rimmed example at Beaulieu that year and whilst on a visit to a food factory (I was a writer by then, having escaped the classroom), I mentioned my interest in old cars to those showing me around. They had the engineering skills and were happy to machine a billet of aluminium that served as a boss and locator for the wheel. I've always found it useful to cultivate the friendship of engineering departments . . .

The Hamblin became a fine weather car simply because there was no obvious way to attach a hood to it. Just about everyone I met who saw the car asked what it was and, like the Super Acc, it was never a chore having to recount the car's history. Unlike that of the Super Acc, this car was not particularly well-documented and the Hamblin was basically another example of a company seeing an opportunity for supplying a Special to the market in the postwar era. Fibreglass was getting into its stride by then and the Hamblin wasn't alone in the Specials marketplace. In fact, in retrospect, these were the last gasps of the Austin 7-based Special, for time had moved on and a car was more accessible to a larger part of the population. Interest in transport with pre-war underpinnings was growing weaker as motoring was becoming a more sophisticated pursuit.

What might have been the bee's knees for a twenty-something in the 1950s would no longer cut the ice by the next decade.

A low, smooth profile gave the Hamblin a much more timeless look than earlier Specials: it could even be considered attractive in a certain light

CHAPTER EIGHT

The Metropolitan Line

1961 Austin Nash Metropolitan

All the while the Hamblin was exploring the byways of Kent, the Met was languishing in a garage. The Scimitar provided my daily transport and the third car, as usual, was being neglected.

When I'd bought the Metropolitan on the rebound, as it were, I was very excited at the prospect of restoring this car to its former glory. There was something special about these cars, the bulk of which were exported to the US, since the Nash was designed to be a small town car for the Americans. History, of course, dictated otherwise and our American cousins would continue their deep-rooted love-affair of transport that could seat three abreast up front and which relied on nothing smaller than a V8 under the bonnet.

The best adjective to sum up the Metropolitan would be that of "cheeky". In convertible format it's great fun for those who are not in a hurry

The Nash, then, was a curiosity with a capital C. To many, I suspect, it was the 1950s personified in some respects yet the cars were dead in the water by 1962. Its transatlantic styling was cute, though, with that highly distinctive two-tone bodywork, separated by an elongated Z-shaped chrome strip. Everything was over white: black made a dramatic statement; pink didn't look out of place; red was available and there was pale yellow as well as the turquoise I'd turned up. Cut-down rear fins accentuated the US link and lavish use of chrome again reinforced the car's target audience. Moreover, there was a column-mounted, three speed gearshift to keep things user-friendly for those across the pond.

Inside, the convertible (unlike the coupe) was at best a two seater with some space behind for small persons (but none at all with the hood folded). Trim was invariably black and white and the dashboard a stark, all metal item, containing the inbuilt radio: happily, there were just enough dials and switches to keep you interested. The later cars (like mine) had a bootlid, which sounds odd until you realise that the earlier cars had to be loaded from within: a strange oversight on the part of Austin. Doors were a very clever design feature, though: they were symmetrical in shape and so could be swapped from the left to the right hand side, had you the desire to do so. Under the bonnet was the trusty (in my case rusty) Westminster 1500 engine, underlining the British heritage of this rather odd hybrid.

My latest acquisition was not exactly pristine: the rot shown here at the base of the door wasn't localised at all

My Met had been partially dismantled by the chap who'd bought her at auction. The hood frame had been taken off, cleaned up and painted; the radio had been overhauled and some new cards had been sourced for the doors. Beyond that, though, little had occurred to Basil, as he was known, because of the BAL number plate. There was rust just about everywhere and clearly a fair bit of money was going to be required to get this beauty back on the road again. The club's meagre newsletter contained occasional small ads for spares but there was extremely little about: I would later learn that the spares situation was much healthier in the US. But restoring the car didn't require many special skills or parts: the car ran on proprietary Austin hardware and was of pretty simple construction. It merely required cash throwing at it . . .

Historically, I'd always been in the situation where buying something restored was out of my league yet the possibilities afforded by restoration were infinitely more accessible. And so it was with the Met: I never did scrape up enough in the way of resources to finish, let alone start, the job and to my intense disappointment, the Met forecast remained dull and cloudy. I did acquire sales brochures relating to the Metropolitan as well as a workshop manual, but that was just about all.

I reluctantly had to pass her on when the next classic attraction beckoned.

(As a footnote, two decades on from the sale, I came across this very same car, which had just been sold, through a contact with the Metropolitan club. Yes, I was considering getting back into Met ownership, only to find that these cars were now scarcer than hen's teeth.

And Basil *still* hadn't been restored . . .)

Looking for all the world like a giant Airfix kit, Basil awaited restoration and re-assembly. And waited . . .

. . . for an investment that would have given him a new lease of life, as witnessed here by a similar car sighted at Beaulieu

CHAPTER NINE

Norfolk mustard

1970 Lotus Europa S2

When you've cherished a dream for years and years and the time finally comes to realise it, one of two things happens. First, the love of your life turns out to be hopelessly artificial, something akin to a girl who relies on too much make-up and the depth of whose extended conversation wouldn't allow a fly to dampen its feet; or, that the selected beauty is more than skin-deep and actually fulfils, nay exceeds, all the necessary criteria.

A Lotus, I have to say, can be both . . . at once.

Whilst I was working in France on my year abroad as part of my degree, I assiduously purchased all the available Brooklands Reprint books on Lotus. These I got to know by heart during the long quiet evenings that I passed in my room, devoid of any entertainment save a cassette radio.

These books fed my imagination, not that it needed much sustenance. I was earning a modest amount in my teaching job, which was being supplemented by private lessons outside of the school. Moreover, my calculations led me to believe that on returning to Blighty (the year was 1982) I'd have around £2,000, enough to buy the Lotus Europa of my dreams.

Dreams, though, are intangible, frustrating things, aren't they? My plans came to naught as I had a degree to finish and the supposed funds never quite came up to expectation.

A decade and a bit later, though, things had changed. The prospect of Lotus ownership was tantalisingly on the horizon. All I had to do was sell my Reliant Scimitar and, since it was now getting to the stage that its value was depreciating quite rapidly (a factor accentuated by the car's unpopularity), I deemed it an opportune moment to part company. A buyer was (eventually) found and the Nash Metropolitan was disposed of, too—which left me ready to contemplate Lotus ownership. A company car made all this possible: after all, no-one runs a Lotus on a daily basis, do they?

I then began to realise that twin-cam ownership, my ideal, was still annoyingly out of my league. House purchase and all the other concomitant realities of married life rendered my overall budget modest: the best I could hope for would be a Renault-engined example.

The distinctive sloping roofline of the S2 Europa: later, twin-cam cars would have this profile modified for better visibility

The bit between my teeth, I quickly drew up a shortlist. Three S2 cars were located; all were in Carmen Red; and one was just ten miles away. The local example I visited first. This car wasn't quite standard, though, having a 1647cc Renault engine mated to a Renault 365 gearbox that allowed five gears and not four. It had been black before but the respray was fine; the chrome bumpers were a little rusty; the wheels lacked the distinctive Lotus hubcaps and the dashboard was delaminating. It was also lopsided (a common characteristic that is remedied by judicious application of penny washers in the suspension).

It looked pretty, though, and drove well enough but I had to see the other two. As was the norm with all my purchases of unusual cars, this entailed travelling. One was in Wetherby, in Yorkshire, the other in Stockton-on-Tees. Helen and I took her Polo one day and we did them both.

It was a long day.

To cut an uninteresting story short, the other two cars carried the standard 1.4-litre engines but had been cosmetically modified here and there, which didn't appeal to me. This was becoming a problem with older cars by now: less than scrupulous owners were tarting them up or transforming them, adding bigger tyres and suchlike. All well and good: but Colin Chapman's idea of the Europa was pure and simple and it didn't need anything adding or subtracting from it. It was perfect from the start.

Coming back to Kent I realised that the one to have was the local car and, despite the above-mentioned shortcomings, it represented a sound buy. The little jobs would be attended to in the fullness of time and I'd derive my usual pleasure from carrying out the corrections. And thus began my love affair with Lotus.

Lots Of Trouble, Usually Serious is the acronym explanation that owners like to toss about when it comes to running Norfolk's pride and joy. I became part of the just-formed local owner's club, taking the job of secretary and treasurer since I could write (!) and our little group grew as time passed.

As for my Europa it was, as usual, a question of attending to those little jobs. The bumpers were removed and taken off to my trimmer-cum-chromer. I located four new hubcaps and even found four steel wheels at a car show. The design of these was peculiar to the early Lotuses and I kept one for a spare and sold the others for a profit. A friendly garage allowed me access to their ramp so I was able to get the suspension levelled.

Tragedy and frustration, though, were never far away when it came to the Europa. I carefully re-fitted the bumpers, took the car for a run down to the local shops and whilst there, someone in a van reversed into the car. The driver claimed not to have seen the Lotus. There was a tiny dent on the ridge of the bumper but nothing more. I left it at that but the reaction was delayed—it always is with fibreglass. A week later a little crack appeared in the paintwork. I was really annoyed but could do nothing about it. After all, I assured myself, you can't keep cars in cotton wool.

The stunning shape of the Europa was also highly practical, since the car benefited from a very low coefficient of drag

That said, the Europa was now looking good again and only one job remained: the dashboard. Since this is the prime focus inside the car, it's difficult to avoid staring at a tatty dashboard. I put my name down for a replacement (it's only plywood with a veneer but only one specialist was producing them), and waited. And waited. If you wanted originality it was a question of patience. I'd found out that to have someone swap the dash would have cost over £100, which was money I could ill afford, so I determined to do the job myself. It was only when I was halfway through the task that I realised just what I had undertaken—and why experts charge so much.

A Bank Holiday weekend was selected for the transformation process and, armed with spanners and an endless supply of labels (for every single wire would have to be annotated), I started the operation. It took ages simply to free off the steering column from its mounts because the bolts only permit a slight spanner turn before you have to remove the spanner and recommence. Yes, it's true, everything on a Lotus is user-unfriendly.

A neighbour passing the row of garages kindly offered to help, which was a boon—whilst two people can't do much together in the confines of a Europa cockpit, the moral support and advice is worth its weight in gold.

It was a pain—literally—changing that dashboard within the compass of an ordinary garage. You have to work upside down at peculiar angles, freeing off instruments and undoing this and that. Finally I had the dash off, instruments in a box, and was left with a mass of spaghetti bearing cryptic notes on scraps of sticky label. It was a sight to unnerve the stoutest of restorers.

In all, it took me three days to effect the changeover. I also spoiled the long-awaited new dash: a couple of tiny holes had to be drilled into the back but in my exuberance at making the first, the drill went straight through and came out the other side. This hole had to be judiciously covered with a Lotus lapel badge. As I've said elsewhere, car DIY wasn't my strong point.

Once the gauges were back in I had to check all was well. It was, save that the fuel gauge didn't seem to function correctly, leading to me having to guess fuel levels thereafter. In fact, it was simply a misrouted wire but I didn't find this out until some months later, at which point I corrected the error. The work had been worthwhile, though, and the car's interior was now lovely, those reclined seats complemented by the brand new dashboard.

Being mid-engined, the Europa was incredibly sure-footed. I always worried about engine cooling, though, which was known as the car's Achilles Heel

But no-one ever said Lotus ownership was easy.

This fact was hammered home one day when I inadvertently left one of the window winder rocker switches in the ON position. The pair lie in little recesses, surrounded by chrome, in the central tunnel which is made of very thin vacu-formed plastic. Because their fit was always a little injudicious, it was an easy mistake to make. The result I discovered a few days later when next I tried to lower the driver's window: nothing. In fact, the motor had burned out, so that meant a replacement.

Most owners of 1960 and 1970s Lotus know that with spare parts it's a case of identifying the original product. Coin Chapman was a master at making do: after all, it was far cheaper to raid someone else's parts bin for bits that would have necessitated expensive tooling and production. The Europa is typical of the breed: the front bumper comes from a Ford Anglia, for example. Insofar as the electrics went, Chapman believed that powered windows were as cheap to fit as the manual variety, provided that a suitable motor could be found. Once again Ford supplied the necessary part, in this case a windscreen wiper motor from the ubiquitous Anglia. I was (as usual) lucky enough to track down a classic Ford parts dealer and secure one of these items which, for a change, was fairly straightforward to fit once the door card had been detached. After that I always checked my rocker switches with a fanaticism bordering on the insane.

Out of the garage, though, the Lotus was everything that I thought it would be—and more besides. It was (and remains) the only car I've ever had that can take a local twisty hill whilst you change up through the box and not down. Those extra cc made a big difference, giving me a taste of the twin-cam version although the car's gently sloping roof extensions singled it out as an earlier model.

Came the big day, and our annual French holiday. I eschewed the company Peugeot 205 in favour of the S2. We put all our worldly possessions into plastic carrier bags and filled the rear and front stowage trays. The S2 doesn't accept conventional suitcases, you see. As a last-minute thought I popped into the nose a little bag containing a sponge and chamois: I've always been an inveterate polisher, probably occasioned by the sort of cars that I've owned. Well, you've probably noted by now, they *do* tend to attract a bit of attention.

We also took a belt and braces insurance cover that gave us the use of another car in case of need.

In retrospect, it was the addition of that last little bag that was to prove our downfall.

We crossed the Channel quite happily, hit Calais and set off towards Paris. An hour or so into France a strange smell assailed my nostrils but it vanished after a few miles, so we carried on regardless. Another hour passed and we arrived on the Boulevarde Périphérique. We slowed as the traffic began to build and finally stopped in a queue. That was when I noticed smoke issuing from the rear of the car.

It's not one of the best sights in the world, smoke coming out of the rear louvres over the bonnet, but this Lotus was venting (literally) its fury at being held up in a jam. We limped off at the first exit and I turned off the engine to try and establish what had happened. Overheating, obviously. A peek under the front lid revealed the enormity of the problem. My little bag had blown into the fan and knocked it out. That had been the smell, of course; now, with no air getting through, the engine was cooking. I telephoned for breakdown assistance and explained in French the problem. At the mention of the word Lotus I could almost see the mechanic shrugging his Gallic shoulders but I was able to assure him that the car had a Renault fan, so a replacement of that ilk would probably do the job.

We waited for hours before he finally turned up with a selection of fans, one of which he fitted. By this time it was mid-afternoon so we re-joined the traffic and drove slap into another jam. About a mile further on the problem recurred—more smoke. That settled it—I got out and called for the breakdown services to come and take the car away. Whilst awaiting the pick-up Helen, fatigued and stressed beyond the pale, threw up at the side of the road. The truck appeared, picked up the Europa, and deposited the pair of us at the nearest cheap hotel, of the Balladin chain. You can perhaps imagine the sight as we walked up to the reception desk, clutching an assortment of plastic supermarket bags . . .

Helen went straight to bed; I partook of a huge meal and a bottle of wine and the following day we collected our left-hand drive Corsa and proceeded on our way to the Cevennes, where we had a perfectly lovely time and never looked under the bonnet once. Somehow, on the way back and without sat nav, we found the Parisian garage, collected the S2 (which had created a lot of interest over the fortnight) and drove back to the UK.

Now people are funny folk and many have an aversion to driving in a particular country. Well, for my part, I can tell you quite categorically that, having broken down in an old Lotus on the Paris ring road, life holds no further horrors for me.

The M25?

Reader, I laugh at it.

On another occasion we took the S2 across to the Nord Pas de Calais to stop at a friend's cottage for a few days. This initial trip, performed in April, cemented an interest in the area that has seen us return pretty much every year since and even investigate the possibility of buying a little place in this largely agricultural region. We visited the tiny (as was) museum of Agincourt whilst there and waited patiently for a group of schoolchildren to leave the main room, which housed a diorama showing, with plastic figures, the effects of the English longbow on the flower of French chivalry. The youngsters were suitably awestruck by the teacher's explanation and then the teacher noticed us waiting to view the scene. "Attention, les Anglais" she murmured to the group who parted with precipitation, still mindful, I fancy, of the outcome of the battle!

The S2 spent most of its time in the UK, however. One highlight was that mine was the actual car representing the Renault-powered Europa that appeared in "The Lotus Book" by William Taylor. My S2, at the time, was one of the few early cars on the road and Lottie was duly accorded two pages of glorious technicolour. She looked quite magnificent.

With the S2 now as I wanted her, the time had come once more to cast around for something else to enjoy. I was missing the sun again; and having a deep-rooted liking for open air transport, it behoved me to find something that would satisfy that end. A garage local to me usually had a range of oddball cars and at the time that I was looking, there was something in stock that appeared to fit my criteria.

Moreover, it was French . . .

CHAPTER TEN

Another French affair

1967 Renault Caravelle

Up to now you'll have noticed, dear reader, assuming that you haven't nodded off, that I've been pretty faithful to the British car industry. That has not come about through chance: the fact is, when it's a question of old cars, the British heritage is one that is unrivalled and, dare I say it, the envy of the civilised world. Having been blessed with the Industrial Revolution before anyone thought of harnessing steam power, the seeds for a fertile future in the manufacturing sector were sown: and in particular, the sector that would offer four wheels and a variety of body styles. It doesn't matter where else you look; for the car enthusiast, the UK has a rich seam that rewards continued mining. Which was exactly what I was doing.

My divergence from things British really came about through the fact that open air motoring was my priority and that I couldn't find anything that actually interested me. Oh, there were plenty of soft-tops for sale (and I'm the sort of chap who'd buy a ragtop in December) but what I was after was something cheap yet reasonably practical: in other words, not another Austin 7.

The small ad for a local country garage showed, *inter alia*, a 1900s Renault road sweeper for sale (!) but of greater interest to me was the Renault Caravelle. The car I knew a little about, but had to confess that I'd not seen one on the roads for decades. With its sister, the Floride (essentially a smaller-engined facsimile), this car was quite a rarity by the 1990s. Why, exactly, is hard to say. I imagine that not that many were sold over here (it was, after all, the Renault Dauphine in a party frock, as one motoring journalist memorably wrote some years back) and the dreaded rust had ravaged many of those that remained on the roads here. Whatever the reason, they very rarely surfaced—and the one at the garage was probably typical of most of the survivors.

Poles apart, yet sharing an engine from the same French company, the Europa and Caravelle made for interesting bedfellows

Finished in a deep plum red, possibly Minervois, possibly Medoc, the car was basically sound although it exhibited tell-tale bubbling here and there, denoting that the steel wasn't that happy underneath its patina. It came with both a soft-top and a hardtop; a single radio speaker (ah, the halcyon days of mono!) and an excellent interior (including a pair of scarce, orange-tinted plastic sunvisors). One downside was that the bumpers were both holed and rusty. There was a reasonable boot (up front, of course, this being a rear-engined car) and the engine, though of modest proportions at 1100cc, was enough to propel the *boulevarde* cruiser at a reasonable rate. I appreciated the crisp styling and mini-transatlantic look of the thing; and it goes without saying that its rarity also appealed. For a pottering-about car on sunny days, it fitted the bill admirably.

I drove it for a few months with the hardtop *in situ* but was really waiting for the first chance to remove it. I've never liked hardtops nor ever have I sought them: one came with the 1800ti Scimitar all those years back but I sold it without ever seeing it. If you buy a convertible then it's for use with the top down—that's all there is to it. I never cease to be amazed by the sight of Brits tootling around in 30°C with their ragtops firmly up: once the temperature gets above 16°C, I'm all for the open air. And with some of my cars, a sheepskin jacket and a flying helmet has meant that I could enjoy them all year round, which is even better.

A rare sight in the UK, the Caravelle always provoked comment, since most people had never seen one

So what was the Caravelle like to own? For a local trip car, it was perfect. We squeezed the family Spaniel into the rear seats and the spacious interior (a flat floor, thanks to an absent transmission tunnel, lent it extra girth) was very welcoming. You couldn't take it around bends at speed, though, for the roll factor was up there with a 2CV on top of a jelly. Basically sound and easy to drive, the Caravelle entertained us both. However, just before the first Christmas of ownership the water pump failed, so that meant changing it, which wasn't a problem but the task wasn't aided by the freezing cold weather, I recall. I was also on the look-out for replacement bumper sections and even rear light lenses, which were peculiar to these models. That summer we holidayed in southern France and I scoured scrapyards for such items but without success. Then, a few months later, a dealer I had met in Montpelier contacted me to say that he'd found a brand new middle section for the rear bumper, which was the main area of trouble. This was an amazing discovery and so I was then able to detach all six sections and take them to my trimmer/chromer for repair and renewal. Another acquaintance made a small run of rear lenses of varying quality, some of which I passed on to Renault Club members.

Those big bumpers occupied a lot of my spare time: finding replacement sections was no easy job

The Caravelle never returned to its maternal home, though, remaining firmly on British shores, which was probably just as well since a little while later the engine started playing up. Closer inspection by way of a compression test revealed that one cylinder was drastically down so a rebuild became necessary. I can't say that this actually transformed the car's performance but it did look a whole lot tidier under the bootlid after the operation. The car attended a few local car shows and was usually mistaken for an Amphicar. This really intrigued me: whilst I could discern a slight resemblance, I'm certain that only a tiny number of people have ever seen the ultra-rare Triumph-powered car-cum-boat. It's the same with the Westfield X1 that I currently own: its assymetrical rear, caused by the Le Mans fairing, puts people in mind of the D-type Jaguar. And just how many people have ever seen one of *those*?

Undeniably good-looking, the Caravelle was pleasingly proportioned and could accommodate four easily

Owning the Caravelle led me into joining the Renault Club where, after a few months, I started to co-edit the club magazine. This was to go on for several years until a difference of opinion caused me to relinquish the reins. We did pick up an award for the magazine during my time at the wheel, so that was most gratifying. I also managed to get my hands on a Renault Sport

Spider for a few days, which made for an interesting comparison with Lotus's new Elise.

But things never stand still, do they? By this time I had driven a wide variety of other cars for my freelance writing purposes and of all those that had been borrowed, one stood out head and shoulders above the rest: Caterham's 7. I'd managed to scrounge about five before I finally decided that to have one permanently in the garage was the only possible way to go. With the factory down the road and two or three dealers within an hour's drive, there was plenty of choice.

Consequently, the Europa was sold to a most unlikely-looking would-be Lotus owner (he drove it in winkle picker shoes, for goodness' sake, on the test drive) but the Caravelle proved a sticking point. In fact, the Caravelle turned out to be the only car that I wasn't able to sell—even the obscure Hamblin Cadet found a buyer in the end. By then I'd located a 1700 SuperSprint at a dealership near London and, after a lot of chatting and bargaining, he took the Caravelle in part exchange. We drove back in the Caterham, with Helen compromised in the passenger seat because of a long, stiffening brace that the previous owner had fitted and which terminated in the footwell.

I didn't mind, though, for I'd joined the *élite*.

Ben, our Spaniel, was the principal occupant of the rear seats in the Caravelle

CHAPTER ELEVEN

No more The Prisoner

1990 Caterham SuperSprint

Let's not beat about the bush here: with 135bhp under the bonnet and a selection of goodies that included the competition exhaust and heavier roll bar, this 7 had all the answers. Any boy racer would give his eye teeth for a Caterham which is, in essence, the refined flowering of the Lotus 6 and 7 of yore. A Lotus dealer, Graham Nearn, had bought the manufacturing rights from Colin Chapman back in 1974 when the latter was taking Lotus upmarket, a sector in which the raw, unrefined Lotus 7 didn't really feature. I'd already driven a Lotus 6 and the Lotus 7; the Caterham range, though, was a much better bet since the original idea had simply been improved and made even more drivable.

If that was at all possible.

But let's make no mistake about it: you don't go and buy a Caterham for anything less than sheer driving pleasure.

My first chance at driving one came whilst still teaching at a private boys' school in Kent. The car had been a SuperSprint and at the time had come from the company's garage at the top of Caterham Hill. I recall the rather basic amenities there (the enterprise is now located in a much more affluent building at the bottom of the hill) which comprised a pound, enclosed by wire fencing, in which lay an assorted bunch of cars, all of which were covered in dead flies. On commenting on this unusual preparation procedure I was informed that the cars didn't hang around long enough to be cleaned . . .

Our first borrowed car, finished in Post Office Red, confirmed our interest in Caterham's alternative transport

Anyhow, Helen and I drove the car back home for the few days' test, got caught in a rainstorm at Westerham and quickly found that to get the hood up you needed to unbolt the rear wheel. Of course, there was no spanner in the car. Caterham owners have to be a hardy (and enterprising) bunch, we quickly agreed.

That week passed as if in a dream. The enticing vision of the red car in the garage meant that it was pressed into service at every opportunity and we relished every minute spent with the car. The report, duly penned, included a quote from Helen to the effect that everyone should have a little red sports car in their garage: a quote that I would use, in later times, to persuade her that my next intended purchase was, really, quite a sane one after all.

Another SuperSprint, this one in Canary Yellow, featured modified front indicators on rubber stalks, one of which can just be seen on the nose cone. Thankfully Caterham dropped the idea

Other Caterhams followed on a loan basis, since I was always happy to pen a few words on behalf of the Surrey-based company. I had actually made the acquaintance of Graham Nearn and his wife by this time through a most extraordinary set of circumstances. My school had invited Graham to give the end of term pep talk to the boys and he duly turned up in a Caterham, as did his wife. The headmaster, knowing my interest in such vehicles, introduced me and somehow I ended up taking boys around the block all afternoon in one of the cars that had come along. I couldn't ever recall being as high: the last time was probably when I'd won, with a colleague, the darts championship at university one evening. Anyhow, such occasions as that become simply indelible.

Helen demonstrates how not to exit a Roadsport with the hood up – and models some inappropriate footwear into the bargain

Later, we would take a Roadsport to France on the hovercraft for a long weekend in November (and still managed to get the top down for a day). That was enormous fun, especially with a six speed box, which caused a lot of head scratching over which gear to select for whizzing around roundabouts. Less wonderful was another car I borrowed which I managed to spin through 180 degrees on the way back to the factory after negotiating a damp roundabout. The car came to rest, thanks to a lamp post, which showed scant regard for the vehicle's offside rear wing. I walked on to the factory where, sheepishly, I explained the predicament to one of the bosses, who ran me back down to the spot to check over the car. I ended up paying the (discounted) repair bill (which fortunately happened to coincide with a building society payout that very week) but the most embarrassing bit was that the car hadn't even been a press vehicle—it had just been built by an employee! This latter was most magnanimous about it, though, inferring that such things happen in the course of Caterham ownership. I was much more cautious thereafter.

Made it! A lot of alloy to polish made initial Caterham ownership a bit of a headache, but that was secondary to the fun factor

Anyhow, I digress. Having my very own Caterham was wonderful. The only thing I disliked about the car was its wheels: these were standard pattern alloys for the time but were very similar to those sported by Skodas. A conversation with one of the Caterham managers led to the unearthing of four, quad spoke green Revolution alloys, which looked much better. Sad to say, I never got around to fitting them.

There was one other nuisance with this car: because it was semi-painted, there was a lot of bare alloy. This stuff looks great when the car is new but after a few years' driving, with exposure to all sorts of road material, the sheen goes and strange marks appear. To get rid of these imperfections the alloy has to be taken back and polished up, which is a long old job. I did my best with various compounds but the car always looked a little jaded, despite strenuous efforts.

There was also little to add to the Caterham package: I invested in a luggage rack (although with hood up, the boot space wasn't that bad) and I also bought a hood roll, a fabric sausage that sat on the rear of the car and contained the hood when not in service.

If there is one drawback to Caterham ownership, it's that hood. Since most people don't want it up (firstly, because this is a car to be driven open and secondly, because entry calls for unusual gymnastic contortions with the hood in place), its natural place is that of being stowed in the rear, in an envelope. This is all well and good—until you need it in an emergency. By then, the hood has shrunk a little through cold and being compressed. And to compound matters, if it's raining, then it's likely to be so cold that the hood won't stretch easily. Throw into the equation something that's a tight fit at the best of times (and which requires superhuman strength to fit over certain poppers), add wetness and you end up with a situation that at best is impractical, at worst impossible. If you *do* manage to get the hood attached, you'll be soaked through long before the process is completed. The simple fact is that hoods are almost mere decoration once they've been folded away for any length of time. If you are ever lucky enough to get one erected, the result is a snug interior with plenty of headroom, though.

As with most of my cars, the Caterham duly took us to France, where we seldom saw another example. It caused, as again with most of my transport, plenty of interest from a country bereft of classic sports cars. Its torque and sheer roadholding I greatly appreciated and with the wide open roads of northern France, with few police about and even fewer traffic lights, the car was really in its element. For a week's holiday it sufficed, for we were *sans enfants* at that time: and although it had to be parked outside, the downpours and damp didn't seem to affect it one whit, thanks to a tonneau.

My period with the SuperSprint was uneventful, to be honest, and aside from regular polishing and oil changes, nothing much had to be done. I was settling happily into long term ownership when the subject of a house move came up: to effect the move into an older, more characterful house, we'd require every penny.

My local Lotus club yielded an interested purchaser and the SuperSprint was easily sold, along with those spare wheels which, with hindsight, I should have hung on to.

But I didn't.

Moreover, we didn't move, either.

After three houses fell through in the area in which we were interested, suddenly the opportunities dried up, so we called it a day. I found myself with nothing in the garage, a state of affairs that had to be quickly rectified. What I really wanted after the Caterham was another Lotus, an Elan to be exact. However, prices were exorbitant for these cult cars, so that avenue seemed closed.

But then there was an alternative, to my mind, that would serve me equally well.

The good things in life? The Caterham was perfect for car shows
(and was just able to accommodate a modest picnic basket)

CHAPTER TWELVE

The Adams family

1967 Marcos 1650

Marcos, you may recall, was not a marque exactly unknown to me. From time to time I'd sighted one of these gorgeous coupes on the road. The Marcos of the 1960s and 1970s was arguably the most beautiful closed two-seater ever made, although I think that competitors for the accolade would have to include the Lotus type 95 Elite and Lamborghini's Miura. The Marcos was perfect from any angle: a long, phallic bonnet terminated at the base of a raked screen; the roof line dipped imperceptibly to the rear wraparound window, which in turn fell away slowly to the cut off tail, the rump of which sported a vestigial spoiler. Cut-outs under the cockpit allowed the occupants to sit even lower than usual and instead of an adjustable steering wheel or sliding seats, the pedal box could be moved backwards or forwards via a little wheel on the dash. A neat solution to the standard problem of how to accommodate drivers of different heights, *n'est-ce pas?*

At the car's debut, the 1964 Racing Car Show, the 1800 model was the talk of the town and subsequent purchasers included pop stars and celebrities. Small wonder, really, for here was a vehicle that stopped you dead in your tracks.

Whilst we had the Scimitar 1800ti I'd dropped by the Marcos factory (well, Nissen Hut complex) in Wiltshire with Helen one day to do a write-up on Jem Marsh's creation. In fact Jem, as is well-known, was only one third of the Marcos formula: the styling proper came from the draughtboard of one Dennis Adams (who was behind various unusual cars of the era), whilst Marcos itself also relied on part of the surname of Frank Costin, an ex-de Havilland engineer who was to use his aerodynamics background in modifying and enhancing other cars, quite apart from those that he designed himself, such as the Costin.

Jem Marsh's 1990s Marcos marked a departure from the traditional coupe concept: fresh air motoring was available at last

There I drove the latest Marcos, which by the 1990s was sporting slightly more bulbous bodywork and a bigger engine: the shape was still largely there but it was somewhat akin to an ageing screen star who was beginning to lose her looks. Nonetheless, it was still a highly attractive vehicle and the example I drove, in typical Jem Marsh fashion, had no registration plate attached on the rear. To atone for this (and just in case we ran into a policeman who'd never heard of the car manufacturer), Jem quickly affixed a chrome Marcos bonnet badge over the number plate holder before we set off. Helen followed in the Scimitar (in the hood arrangement of which Jem had expressed an interest) and later had to wade into a ditch to retrieve the chrome badge that had fallen off the Marcos. I recall Jem being annoyed at the scratched badge upon being presented with it, for this had involved unnecessary expense! I then took my photographs and we parted.

That day lingered in my memory to the point that now I felt a Marcos would be something to cherish. New cars were way out of my league and anyhow, I was more interested in the classic side of the equation. Once again, I joined the relevant club and the hunt was on. In fact, few ever came to market: owners obviously enjoyed these cars and they were thus seldom up for grabs.

Finally, the long-awaited small ad appeared: a chap in London had not one but *two* of the cars for sale. I couldn't wait to get over to view. His tandem garage did indeed contain two cars, one, from 1967, in metallic pale blue, the other a 1970 car in red. It was like visiting Aladdin's cave: to have the choice of two cars was gilding the proverbial lily, and then some.

Low and mean, the Marcos shape was an historic milestone and still turns heads decades later

I actually didn't need to spend long on the choice. The 1967 car was the purer design of the two and incorporated the little things that made a Marcos so special to me. The twin, round headlights were one factor (the later cars went for single oblongs, which didn't look right) whilst the rear clusters, from a Vauxhall Victor, looked prettier than the rectangular lenses of the 1970s car. Moreover, the gearshift of the earlier car was a better affair: I believe that later cars had something derived from the Ford Transit, which was nowhere near as slick.

Whilst I was sampling the blue car the owner asked Helen which car she thought I'd prefer. Helen had no doubts—she knew me too well by this stage—and replied that the earlier car would be perfect for my criteria.

This, in fact, turned out to be true, although its purchase involved me taking on two cracks along the huge bonnet and a colour scheme that I didn't much care for (I've always preferred non-metallic paintwork). Another sliver of paint was missing from the rear Kamm tail, too. That aside, I inherited side windows that relied on slackening off a knurled nut so that they dropped into the doors; seats that were the most comfortable of any car I've ever driven; a rare engine conversion from the hands of Chris Lawrence (one of just 32); a wooden chassis (tubular steel came later); and a shape that simply couldn't be improved upon. To add to this already impressive list was a welcome fabric sunroof (my love of the open air would never diminish) and wire wheels, which really set the whole car off. Oh, and 120bhp, which gave the car plenty of performance, too.

How many cars look this good from this angle? A Kamm tail completes the carefully penned design

Back home, I started getting to know the car and duly wrote an article for the owners' club. More would follow. The car, with its enlarged 1650cc engine, was a very scarce commodity: Chris Lawrence of Lawrencetune had also souped up Morgans in a similar manner and he had been involved in his own vehicle manufacture with the Deep Sanderson marque. This had never quite got off the ground, which was true of the handful of Deeps manufactured: they were just 36 inches high, making the Marcos at 42 inches seem decidedly tall. Chris was delighted to be reunited with my car when we met by chance some months later, although the meeting was actually part of a trip to a nearby specialist who had been engaged to try and sort out the car's doors.

Ah, yes, those doors.

The old epigram about beauty being only skin deep certainly applied to the Marcos. In true glassfibre fashion it was at once fabulous and fragile, and would provide me with hours of tinkering, as unlikely things started to go wrong . . .

The doors were a case in point. Doors on Marcos cars of this age seldom fitted very well, often sitting proud of the bodywork and defying owners' attempts to right them. I wasn't aware of any problems with the car I'd bought until, one day, going around a sharp bend the driver's door opened. This, as you might imagine, is a somewhat unsettling experience. I assumed that the door hadn't been clicked shut properly so pulled it to, only to have the experience recur a little later. Body flex and the wooden chassis were doubtless to blame to some extent.

Back at base I took a look at the door locks and discovered that I couldn't actually lock either door. The captive metal strikers were quite worn and these, it transpired, came off the humble Austin A30. Despite my fiddling and attempts at realignment, I couldn't improve on the situation. At length I located two spare A30 striker plates and then found out that the problem could become so severe that cutting the door in two long-ways and re-glueing it was the only solution. The guru of this art lived down Bath way and so there we headed one weekend.

A week or so later we returned to collect the car, with the job done: it hadn't required the services of a buzz saw, after all. On the way home the low sun presented a problem I hadn't hitherto encountered: it reflected on the almost flat rear screen and dazzled the driver so that I couldn't see what was behind me. Ah, what we put up with in the name of style.

At that particular time the Hamblin was still with us and a local car show was coming up. I decided to take the Cadet along whilst Helen would drive the Marcos. I left home before her on the day since the Austin 7 Special was a bit slower.

I was at the show, parked up in the appropriate slot for a good half-hour before the Marcos put in an appearance. When she had finally parked, Helen was unable to get out of the car, though! Closer inspection revealed why: a length of old string was looped around the top of the driver's door frame and the sunroof aperture. This, Helen explained, was to keep the door from coming open . . .

En route, the heart-stopping moment had re-occurred, about three miles from home. Totally unexpected, there was little she could do—the door just wouldn't click shut, despite the attentions it had undergone at the hands of the Marcos guru. Distraught, she had stood at the side of the road, pondering her next move. Luckily a passing motorist took pity on her (I'd like to think that he was, or had been, a classic car owner) and had stopped to proffer help. Between them they hit on the idea of strapping the door shut (inelegant, I grant you, but efficacious) but this could only be effected by some sort of wire or cord. Who, amongst you I wonder, keeps such items in the boot for emergency?

We certainly didn't.

Anyhow, as luck would have it, a search of the adjacent ditch revealed a length of tatty twine, sufficient to perform the job. Helen thus arrived with the car bound up a bit like a Christmas turkey and didn't win any *concours d'élégance* points at that particular show.

Thereafter, when I had an odd moment, I continued to try and rectify the door situation. I don't think that I ever really solved it: when it seemed to be tightly shut a hefty pull on the handle would cause it to pop open again. Perhaps more rigidity in the base product was required—but I'm not an engineer, so I can't comment further.

The silencer box gave up the ghost a little while after and despite getting the correct box from a specialist, the replacement was just too deep and kept catching the odd undulation. So I tried Kwik Fit for something of a lower profile and helpfully, after a lot of fiddling, they came up with a Volvo item of very shallow depth.

State-of-the-art the factory may not be, but every owner needs at some point to pay homage at the Marcos shrine in Wiltshire

We took the car to northern France once (with not a little trepidation) but she behaved herself well. On one occasion we had stopped at a little sleepy seaside town when a Belgian, on holiday there, saw the car and engaged us in conversation. He asked that we might hang around for half an hour, so that he could rush back to his house and get his camera to take some pictures. It was that kind of car—people stopped in their tracks and looked over their shoulder at us as we drove by. I'm quite sure that virtually no-one in France knows about Marcos, far less has ever seen one.

It was on the way back from Bromley Pageant that year that I was within a mile of home when the wipers failed on the car. I made it back okay but guessed that the mechanism was probably beyond salvage and so another job was added to the car list.

I was able to secure a new mechanism via my club contacts and through talking to people, gained an idea of just what was required to effect the repair. It's a ghastly job, involving partial disassembly of the dash and working half-in, half out of the car. There's little room for manoeuvre; you're constantly at an awkward angle; it's a bit-by-bit process to detach the worm (which in my case had snapped) and the whole thing is covered in grease, of course. Then you have to reverse the whole process: it was a lot like the Europa dashboard saga, I decided. But I managed it and, better still, the wipers worked again.

Snug and superbly comfortable, the Marcos interior was a driver's delight

Marcos and Hamblin ownership came to an end around about the same time because with a small son now a reality, I deemed it wiser to have just one old car. I'd really enjoyed my ownership period with the Marcos, despite all the tribulations, and it's the sort of car that I'd like to own again one day. I have to say that it was more a straight-line speed car than a cornering car in my experience: the Lotus and Ginetta inspired much more spirited driving in that respect. But its scarcity and drop-dead looks atoned for everything. I never did manage to get those cracks in the bonnet sorted out but I did look after the car to the best of my ability: it was finally sold to an enthusiast living in Oz. During my time of ownership I'd met up with Frank Costin, an unassuming chap who lived in a semi-detached house near Northampton. It's hard, looking back, to realise just how skilled and enterprising this fellow was; he was literally streets ahead of his time and contributed many sound ideas to the car industry, including the concept of ground effect, so beloved of the current Formula One scene. He was behind the idea of marine ply for the Marcos chassis, which many ignoramuses derided; but you only have to read up on the history of the de Havilland Mosquito (in books like *The Mosquito Log* by Alexander McKee) to begin to understand the staggering potential of this material.

Sadly, Frank died just six months after I interviewed him. I have both his and Chris Lawrence's dedications in car books as mementoes, however.

Despite all its quirks and eccentricities, a Marcos repays one's ownership. Looking back, my period of custodianship was ultimately rewarding

CHAPTER THIRTEEN

I'm backing Britain!

1971 Lotus Elan coupe

1940 Standard Eight Tourer

It was 1998 and, as mentioned, by now a baby boy had put in an appearance and my life was never going to be quite the same again. A Lotus-owning friend of mine, Andy Burchett, who would later take on my Elan project, summed it up thus: " You lose your life." No-one can ever prepare you for the paternal *rôle* and legion are the stories of enthusiasts who have submitted those dreaded advertisements that begin: "Arrival of baby forces sales of beloved . . ."

I was quite determined that I wasn't bowing out of the old car scene simply because an ankle-biter was in the wings. Fortunately for me, Helen wasn't insisting on a *volte face* insofar as my car interests were concerned and so I was drawn once again to Norwich's prime export. The Elan I'd always admired but prices for 1970s examples were still firm, to put it mildly. The way to proceed, I decided, was via Plus Two ownership.

For reasons that can't readily be explained, the Plus Two had for a long time been the black sheep of the Lotus fold. I can't account for it—I don't think anyone can—but for the purist, only the "Baby" Elan was worshipped. It was as if families and Lotus were not nouns to be mentioned in the same sentence: they were mutually exclusive concepts.

The above-mentioned Andy owned a very presentable Plus Two and he had older children. He assured me that two could still be accommodated at a pinch in the rear of his car. Although I desperately yearned for a little Elan, their prices were totally unrealistic in comparison to the cost of a good Plus

Two. I naturally got to drive his example and, in the words of the protective varnish advert, it did what it said on the tin.

Looking back, far far back, I can recall the advertisements that appeared for the Plus Two in the glossy magazines of the early 1970s. The car looked truly stunning then, and it has since grown old without a wrinkle, a measure of how beautiful the original design was. In 1974, as a gangly sixth-former, I attended the last London Earls Court Motor Show and well recall the Lotus stand. All the cars on display were finished in white: the Elan, the Plus Two and the Europa: the new Elite was just about ready at the time. I knew then that one day I'd own a Lotus . . .

. . . or two.

So, despite what I really wanted, I was going to settle for a Plus Two. This wasn't really the wrench that it might have been: after all, the Plus Two shared the same twin-cam engine as the Baby Elan and it drove and cornered like all Lotus do: on rails.

Cars simply don't come much prettier than the diminutive Lotus Elan that was made up until 1974

That it was incredibly stylish and came (usually) in a dual tone colour scheme were added benefits; additionally, later cars were fitted with a five-speed gearbox, although there were horror stories circulating about the robustness of this latter Maxi-derived fitment. (Come to think of it, there were horror stories circulating on just about every aspect of Lotus ownership, in the main perpetrated by the owners themselves. But that hasn't put people off falling hopelessly in love with these gorgeous vehicles down the years).

The club magazine was for once a happy hunting ground and, as always, it was merely a question of finding the right car at the right price. Despite their bargain basement character, good Plus Twos weren't being sold for birdseed; cars requiring work, such as a new interior or engine rebuild, seemed to be the main contenders. I was adamant that the car I'd buy would have been fitted with a new chassis for whilst some old Lotus were still running around on their existing steel underpinnings, it was generally accepted that after 30 odd years such cars ought to have been re-chassis'd. Steel, unlike fibreglass, does rust, after all.

Things thus became anomalous: I just couldn't locate the right car. In fact I didn't even view one, although I was seduced by a Plus Two cabriolet, a conversion carried out by dealer and parts supplier Christopher Neil. Alas, the car needed work and I wasn't totally convinced that a coupe of the size of the Plus Two was readily adaptable to rag-top guise.

Then, out of the blue, something surfaced in Devon. Yes, again a hike, but here was something that might, at a pinch, solve my predicament. The car in question was a baby Elan coupe and it was half restored. By that, the owner meant that the body had been resprayed, the engine rebuilt and the car had a new chassis. It looked inviting, from both the description and the subsequent telephone conversation.

Andy and I travelled down to Devon to view the car since he had agreed that he would assist in the work to be undertaken: my job, as ever, was to supply the finance and the bits. The seller had several other Lotus cars, a couple of impressive ordinary road cars with personalised number plates, a garden full of granite artefacts that had, in the main, been the handiwork of those spending time at her Majesty's pleasure in the local prison—and a hoist. Now, I've never, ever, been to buy a car and been able to check its underside but here I was in for a treat. Up went the car and we walked about under it, looking for anything suspicious. Surprisingly enough, there was nothing to report: the car obviously belonged to an enthusiast and he was happy to reveal all.

The Elan in Devon was half-restored – but I was not to be put off

In the event it took a year to get to this stage

The car itself was partially reassembled: doors weren't on and likewise, the screen and rear glass were out. There was also a pile of bits in boxes lying inside the cockpit, which lacked carpet, headlining and trim, although the seats were fine. The dashboard was lying in a separate box, along with the (somewhat familiar, by now) array of dials and loose wiring. The spectre of the Europa dashboard saga flitted through my mind. It was, the owner said, all there, for he had done the work himself and simply no longer had the time or inclination to finish the project. A price was agreed and I became the proud owner of my second red Lotus.

Engine had to be checked and overhauled . . .

. . . and it came out of the car more than once because of running problems

Overall, it took just on 12 months to get the Elan through its MOT and back on the highway. It looked, on paper at least, a straightforward job and, by and large, it was. Andy and I fitted in sessions when he was free and this meant, in the main, working at weekends. The suspension was the first thing to finish: Rotoflexes had to be changed and new springs fitted. With the car movable, next came the engine bay, in particular the vacuum operated headlamps. The Elan came with an unfitted period Christoper Neil conversion set-up which we duly attached. Frustration set in when, working out the upper limit of travel of the mechanism, the rotor arm accidentally struck the underside of the bonnet and, you guessed it, caused a star crack. The engine ran, though, so that was good. The dash was duly assembled and fitted; the gearbox was *in situ* and the big things left to do were the headlining and the carpeting. I was able to acquire some star pattern headlining from a trimmer in Birmingham and I managed to obtain a set of headlining steel rods (strangely lacking on the car in question) from a specialist whose arm I had to twist (although I had patronised him in the past). With the glass in, my friendly trimmer then completed the roof and with patterns, made up carpet for the floor. I spent a lot of time locating and glueing from within the little metal devices that held on the chromed strips on the sills before the final carpeting took place. The other big job was the front and rear bumpers: the rear that came with the car fitted well enough but the front example was damaged, so I bought a replacement item. This, my painter found, was a less than perfect fit and required a great deal of fettling to marry up with the chrome strip that separates it from the bodywork. I opted for a gold bumper finish at this point (they should have been silver), just to set off the body colour.

The car completed, we then began to test the engine. The first run lasted only a minute. Andy then ceremoniously unscrewed the oil filler cap and looked at the milky residue that had accumulated. "Water in the oil," was his dreadful diagnosis. (On the Lotus, the Ford block has to be correctly mated to the water pump if you are to avoid this peril. Quite obviously, the last mechanic hadn't done the job properly, so we had to take the engine out). Andy then correctly did the job only to have the same fault recur. Once again, the engine came out. This time the fault was cured (to my enormous relief) and the car was ready to go.

The distinctive Ford-based twin-cam engine, finally happy in situ

Predictably, the actual restoration expenditure had evened out the initial bargain status of the Elan. True, virtually all the parts had been there with the package but the problem was that additional cost was incurred because where there were, for example, two door handles and one was below par, once a replacement was bought, it then made the other look tatty by comparison. So I ended up buying pairs of ancillaries. As ever, there was more to the finishing off than anticipated but at least the Elan was now done and it looked very pretty indeed. These are, in fact, diminutive cars: you only have to see one on a motorway today to appreciate how small they actually are. Inside, however, it's rather like Dr Who's Tardis: there is plenty of room, even for tall drivers.

My first drive around the block (literally) was without tax or MOT but it was a big thrill, feeling the car at last alive under my fingertips. The gearbox, in particular, was very sweet in its action. Writers have compared its movement to a well-oiled rifle bolt and that is a very fair description. I have always believed that the gearshift makes the car: the driving pleasure of anything, however lovely its looks, is impaired by a poor gearchange. Chapman's Elan excelled in this department.

On the day of the MOT the car wouldn't start. With the help of a local car engineer, we traced the problem to a slightly corroded battery earth, nothing more complicated. Earthing Lotus cars was always a touch and go business because there is precious little metal in their composition. However, that fault rectified, the car was duly MOT'd and I began to start enjoying Elan ownership.

At least I did for a few miles. I found that after ten minutes or so at the wheel, the car died. Leaving it to cool solved the problem; the car started and off we went again. Then, the same thing happened. It baffled me and, to an extent, Andy, before it dawned on him that the condenser was failing. Once that was replaced, the Elan behaved impeccably.

Flawed beauty? Although the Elan exhibits quite astonishing roadholding, the behaviour of the Rotoflex coupling arrangement doesn't endear itself to every driver

About this time I felt the yearning for another soft-top. I'd come across a chap living locally who had a restored Standard Flying Eight Drophead and I'd been taken for a ride in it. I'd admired the car's utilitarian yet flowing wartime looks; more importantly, it allowed the sun in, which the Elan didn't, of course.

After a month or two I located a similar car a few towns away, which, as those time-honoured adverts euphemistically say, was "requiring some work". This was actually a sister to the Drophead, the Tourer. The fact was, it was a true classic, made for just a couple of years, so immediately it took my interest, if only for its scarcity value. You'd have thought by now that I'd have learned all my lessons on the restoration front—but no. It wasn't expensive, the bodywork was in primer, all the chromework was detached (but rechromed) and the car required spraying and a degree of reassembly.

Standard Tourer was something of a challenge: bodywork was solid, leaving reassembly the main job

In reality, once I'd purchased it, the only progress that I made on this vehicle was securing the engine data sheets, buying a replacement bakelite dashboard from an autojumble (that turned out to be incorrect anyway) and a lot of poring over articles on the car. The Elan had really drained my finances and so the Standard stayed, well, standard—and resided permanently in the garage.

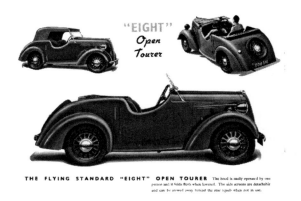

Nostalgia by the bucketful: the Tourer was a dinky little model with heaps of appeal

I should have kept the Elan, having gone to all the trouble of the rebuild. Alas, this idol had feet of clay; or, to be more precise, rubber. In spite of its looks, its handling and its sheer *joie de vivre*, the Elan was flawed to my way of thinking through those famous Rotoflex couplings. It meant the car wound itself up prior to every gearchange and then unwound itself in preparation for the next. Kangaroo progress became the norm—Elan drivers apparently adopt a certain style of driving to cope with this phenomenon. To me, it didn't come easily and whilst I could have changed the Rotoflexes for a different option, I felt that after all the time and money spent, it was probably easier to let the car go.

I took her along to a dealership in Kent for the garage owner to sell on my behalf. The idea was to leave the Elan there and await developments. Whilst performing this operation I took a look around the premises—and fell in love again. Instead of a commission sale I found myself talking part exchanges, having alerted Helen on the phone of the unscheduled change of plan.

As I've observed elsewhere, they're funny things, cars.

What I was aiming at: this example, strangely enough, is finished in the same colour as the car I purchased

CHAPTER FOURTEEN

Back to basics

1991 Caterham 1700 SuperSprint

Another Caterham?

I'm afraid so.

Once the idea of disposing of the Elan had taken root, I realised that the one car that really cut the ice for me was the reincarnation of the legendary Lotus 7. According to the old maxim, you never know what you've got until you no longer have it. No-one could ever say the Caterham was overly attractive and indeed, it would have been interesting to have recorded Frank Costin's thoughts on the shape of the original Lotus 6 and 7. My guess is that he hadn't been impressed by their lack of aerodynamics. Fitted with the flared (or clamshell) wings, the Caterham looked a little more flowing to my mind, so I would have never considered one with simple cycle wings.

The car at the dealership had just arrived. First off, it was bright red all over, so there was no alloy to clean. It came with HPC five spoke wheels and slightly oversized tyres; a competition exhaust; a proper immobiliser and a few other useful extras. I was captivated and didn't need to drive it because the mileage was modest and the dealer well-known to me.

A higher specification SuperSprint than before, Caterham 7 ownership the second time around was even better

A few days later the car sat proudly in one of my garages and life with a Caterham began anew. I suppose that it was a reflection of my tastes that I had come back to Caterham ownership: after all, there were other cars out there. But deep down, as has been explained, I was a Lotus-eater first and foremost and in the Caterham was all that was so special about the marque. It was low, hugged the road like a leech, made a lot of noise and went like the proverbial witch on a broomstick. The acceleration of the SuperSprint left most things in its wake and you really had to spend an awful lot of money on a car to get anything like this kind of performance. Okay, so it had the styling characteristics of a housebrick—but it was a quick housebrick for all that.

I didn't need to settle into Caterham 7 ownership because it all came so naturally to me. It was a blissful time and the only period when SuperSprint ownership palled ever so slightly was when I was lucky enough to borrow Caterham's SuperLight vehicle for a long weekend. If SuperSprint cars were the *ne plus ultra* when it came to four wheel sensations, then I was in for a surprise: Caterham's SuperLight was even more astonishing still.

One glorious weekend saw Charles and I the temporary owners of a SuperLight 500. Other transport pales into insignificance alongside this catapult on four wheels

This vehicle was taken to Bromley Pageant, a huge car show. Driving that car was like nothing else on earth, I have to say. Its six speed gearbox hadn't been told about rev limits and just went from gear to gear without any hiatus at all. The power surge from the 230bhp tuned engine was simply seamless and the car that Caterham ran at the time, in Mango Yellow, was equipped with a tiny wind deflector in place of a proper windscreen. This, along with the unpainted wheels, had the effect of reducing weight but it also played havoc with contact lenses or a sheepskin helmet: this latter would be tugged back over your head through the demonic force of the wind. Keeping your licence with such a car would have also been problematical because of its huge potential: it was a car that simply *had* to be driven quickly.

Honest, officer.

Driving into the Pageant entrance I had to queue and whilst there, a pedestrian passed by, looked at the car, and made an obsequious bow with his body and arms. He, at least, knew all about these vehicles, I decided. I had a whale of a weekend with this *bolide* and it was with enormous reluctance that I took it back on the Monday. I drove into the parking area at the showroom and got out. An older fellow then accosted me and asked what the car was like. I explained that it wasn't mine, but merely borrowed. He expressed surprise at this, for apparently Caterham didn't let anyone drive this model, even if they wanted to order one. And he was awaiting delivery of just such a car.

"You won't be disappointed," was my enthusiastic reply. Had I ever the wherewithal, I decided, the SuperLight would be first on my shopping list.

The 7 is a car that really only warrants being driven with the top down – whatever the weather

My SuperSprint lost some of its gloss after that weekend but it still entertained. I bought a luggage rack only to find that the larger spare wheel prohibited its fitting. A hood envelope was added to take care of the hood and I also invested in a FIA rollbar, since I wanted more weight at the rear in the light of my Torvill and Dean episode in the wet a year or two earlier. The car was regularly tuned although to be fair, the Webers were very reliable and, once correctly set up, did all that was asked of them.

Car shows, polishing and driving became the routine until one year we decided that our annual pilgrimage to France should involve two cars. By this time (2000) we had a daughter. Madame went on ahead with the two infants for three weeks whilst I would follow a week later in the Caterham. Looking back now, these holidays, with two cars in France, were the happiest of times. True, I didn't always get the weather I wanted but on the sunny days, we'd enjoy trips to and from the beach and take turns at the wheel of the SuperSprint. The French loved everything about the car, although this was only to be expected. On the A and B roads, the SuperSprint was truly in its element and as recounted already, there is some superb driving to be had in northern France if you can be bothered to hop across the Channel.

On the first week back after the last holiday spent thus it was sunny so I took the Caterham to work. I had barely got to the end of my road when I noticed flames licking around the cut-out in the panel through which the twin carburettors poke. This was frightening, so I hastily switched off the engine and quickly got out. The fire died away and all settled down. I was pretty rattled by this totally unexpected sight and so drove the car straight home. It seemed fine thereafter so I asked around to see what some of my more mechanically-minded friends thought about this behaviour. The consensus was that the carbs had been over-primed although I wasn't convinced, since I'd always started and driven the car in the same way. Anyhow, that weekend I took her out again to check the *status quo*. We drove about half a mile before, once again, the drama repeated itself. That settled it. I called the breakdown people and had the car taken away to a local garage, feeling lucky that the ignited vapours hadn't developed into something more serious—or that this had occurred a week earlier, when I had been abroad. As it was, I had blistering on the paintwork of the alloy bonnet from the heat build-up and this would have to be sorted out at some point.

The Caterham 7 is one of very few cars that has basically changed little since its inception. In an era of computer-designed lemons, it's a tonic without the gin

Remedial work was carried out and the garage found a split fuel hose between the carburettors: it had simply perished. They attended to some melted wiring and in the meantime I got in touch with a Caterham paintwork specialist to whom I took the offending bonnet. He had a couple of apprentices and used the bonnet as an example of how to repair paintwork without going to the trouble of repainting the whole surface area. He did a remarkable job, I have to admit. Two weeks later the car was back in one piece and all was well.

In closing this chapter, if you're a male and own a Caterham and your partner/ girlfriend/ mistress puts up with it, take my advice and stick with her, for you've found a true soul mate. Any female who doesn't worry about indecorous entry and exit to the car, doesn't mind the odd ankle burn on a hot exhaust and who isn't worried about breaking her fingernails putting the hood over the poppers, has to be worth her weight in that Ratner's merchandise.

CHAPTER FIFTEEN

Wizard—from Oz

1977 Mini Moke

What's the scariest experience you've ever had in connection with buying a second hand car? Buying one under a streetlight at night? Purchasing one that you didn't actually drive before parting with the readies? I can top those: how about buying one *by e-mail*?

I've mentioned that in 2000 we had our second child. Well, the arrival of the said infant did involve a little brokerage, to be honest. I'd asked Helen that if we were going down the dual-child route then I really ought to consider a four-seater soft-top so we could all enjoy the open air. I didn't want arguments developing over who was going in Katie (as the SuperSprint was known) and so on. To my surprise, she semi-agreed to this, which I took as *carte blanche* to go out soft-top hunting.

I actually had a predicament here: the choice of interesting, four-seater topless transport was quite limited insofar as I was concerned. There was the doughty Morris Minor convertible, of course, an example of which I'd borrowed from the chap who'd restored the Super Accessories car. This had been good fun and the car is, of course, a true classic but I didn't like the way the side windows and frames had to stay up: I prefer everything to fold down, for purity's sake. Morris cars of the convertible type were also quite costly.

Again, a Metropolitan was considered but had to be discounted because with the roof down you can't get two in the back. Triumph's Stag was too boring for me; the Caravelle had been done; and other four-seaters in my modest price range were simply without character. Then I recalled an article

I'd written a few years previously when I'd gone to visit Runamoke, a Mini specialist that had premises in Hertfordshire.

All the way from sunny Australia, this particular Leyland Moke quickly adapted to the UK's inclement weather

The Mini Moke was yet another example of British ingenuity and style in a world that seemed, quite often, to be lacking in both qualities. Originally designed for use by the armed forces, the Moke had fallen foul of that sector through ground clearance problems once fully loaded: instead, the military opted for Austin Champs as lightweight troop transport. Thus, in 1964, the Moke drove off the parade ground and into Civvy Street; more exactly, Carnaby Street, where its anti-establishment qualities endeared it to the trendy young things of the Swinging Sixties. Actually, this came about by chance, since the Moke was initially offered as a versatile carrier (the word Moke means donkey, incidentally) to market gardeners and anyone else who had small loads to cart around. For that reason the car was supplied in one of just two colours (green or white). The Moke came with a single seat fitted and no second windscreen wiper, carpets, heater, laminated windscreen, canopy, side doors or even a sump guard. However, these were all offered as options; and like conventional Minis of the time, it was powered by the venerable, if puny, Austin/ Morris 875cc engine. Amongst others, fire brigades and airport services invested in these useful little workhorses but, in time, Mokes came to feature as zany transport in television series and on film sets.

I'd driven an Australian version whilst interviewing the proprietor of Runamoke and had been instantly taken with the car's go-kart like qualities. In fact, the car in question wasn't typical of the genre: it had been endowed with a 1275cc engine and was galvanised, too, thereby representing the apogee of Moke development for many, although I didn't appreciate this at the time. I noted that the Squadron Blue paint was flaking off the car in question but then paint doesn't adhere too well to metal that has been zinc-dipped.

Australian cars were made by Leyland down under from the late 1960s to 1982: some were beefed up, engine-wise, and all were equipped with bigger wheels, so they were far better suited to the outback than their Dinky Toy-like English cousins. In fact, for many Moke devotees, the Oz cars are the best of the bunch in terms of driving. A spell under the aegis of Austin-Rover saw the next generation cars produced in Portugal whilst the final run, which terminated in 1993, were engineered in Italy under the Cagiva label. These last two series all had 1-litre engines and grew more clinical, in keeping with the ever-increasing health and safety regulations: rocker switches replaced pointed Mini switchgear, mundane plastic steering wheels became the norm, roll bars were fitted as standard and so on. In retrospect, the Australian cars offered the most choice (there were three engine sizes, for starters), and they were equipped with more comfortable seats than the English Mokes; most importantly, perhaps, there were plenty made in the 14 year production run.

Trouble was, they were mostly in Australia.

When I resolved on the idea of Moking, it really was the perfect choice. The car could be driven with a couple of the side panels in place or they all could be removed, leaving just the hood up. That could be taken down, if required, and the operation is both simple and quick. The rear seats could also double as luggage capacity, if necessary. The Moke was thus versatility with a capital V.

The difficulty lay in actually finding the right car: British Mokes have been decimated through our damp climate and not that many Oz cars have been brought over. (Although being right-hand drive, of course, they lent themselves to the British enthusiast). Australian cars weren't immune from tinworm, either, but depending on where they were sold, decent cars were about. The club magazine yielded an example from time to time and the handful of dealers (well, three to be exact) also had occasional cars but these carried the usual seller's premium. I knew that English Mokes, whilst the purest of the breed amongst the *cognoscenti*, were not that practical because of their tiny seats and diminutive engines. The Oz cars, as related, suited me much better and so I set my heart on a galvanised example with the bigger engine.

Roof off, and with plenty of room for a quartet, the Moke relishes those long, lazy days of summer

A last, after months of looking, and seeing only a rusty Portuguese example (an early Austin Rover product) and visiting another dealer whose stock was way out of my price range, I got wind of an ex-pat out in Oz who was putting European buyers in touch with Moke sellers in Australia. In actual fact, he'd only completed one deal and mine was to be his last—but I didn't know that. E-mail was in the Brice household by this time and I'd get regular lists from this chap, as and when he found cars. There was everything over there, from semi-wrecks to virtually mint—and in pretty much any colour, too, including brown. Quite who'd fancy a brown Moke was beyond me. Eventually a Devil Yellow Californian example cropped up: it had been restored, had the 1100cc engine (those 1275cc jobs were still eagerly sought after and were more pricey) and it had four seats (two seats and extra luggage space was often preferred in Oz, I noted). I decided to buy on the strength of a wallet of photographs that the chap sent over to me. I duly sorted out a draft via my bank, transmitted it—and waited.

The six week wait coincided with our summer holiday (France again!) and whilst on the beach one day, I had a curious conversation with my wife. She mentioned, quite casually, that there had been an e-mail for me just before we left home. "Something about a car waiting at the docks in Melbourne?"

I couldn't deny this . . .

I had the bills of lading, together with an estimated date of arrival as well as details of the shipping agent. I'd arranged for insurance of the voyage (wouldn't have wanted the car to slip overboard!) and everything was in readiness.

Eventually (and looking back, it could have turned into an absolute nightmare), word reached me that my car was available for collection at Tilbury. I sent off the purchase receipt, one of the bills of lading, a copy of the tear-off part of the logbook and a letter to the UK shipping agent, just to prime them. The boat had finally docked three days late and I then had to choose either to deal with the agent or the customs direct. Dealing with the agent costs you a deferment fee but this means that you pay all the import monies to them and they in turn chase the customs on your behalf for clearance.

There were three bills to pay. The first was Customs Duty on the car, which was typically 10%. You have to declare the car's value and on to this sum is added VAT at 17.5%. Then there were devanning and customs clearance and finally terminal handling, presentation and an agency fee. Presentation, I was to find out, doesn't mean a wax and polish: the Moke was very grimy after her long voyage.

As for the Customs clearance, there was a choice of three ways. My car went down the second route and was cleared in a day.

I enlisted the help of a colleague and he drove me up to the docks to collect the car. I wasn't really sure what to expect for I'd never been to Tilbury before and we both got completely lost. At length, after perusal of a terribly poor photocopy of a terminal map, we found the correct shed and two men, whose office was an inverted, cut-up wooden crate. Upon presentation of the requisite bit of paper, which one of the fellows signed, we were free to return to another shed where a more official form was printed off. This was our exit paper and proof of the vehicle's arrival and clearance.

Predictably, the car wouldn't start but we had come prepared for this eventuality: we had jump leads, along with water, oil, petrol, assorted spanners and so on to try and cover all eventualities. Subsequently, with jump leads attached, much revving of my colleague's car and with plenty of choke and key twisting, the Moke awoke. We left Tilbury, showed our papers at the gate and got home without further ado.

When it had to be fully zipped up, the Moke gave its owner the strange impression of driving in a bin bag

Back home, it was time to assess the car. Inevitably, there were a few things that let the car down. For a start, the restorer had relied on the re-use of many of the original parts. Now, as you'll have learned, I'm all for originality but when, for example, switchgear grows marked and tatty, in my book it can be substituted. Various dashboard addenda were below par in this respect. The car had strange rubber wheel arch skirts, not of the correct Australian pattern; there was a single plastic grab handle for the front passenger in lieu of three metal fitments; and a lot of Aussie anti-smog apparatus under the bonnet. It later transpired that the engine was 998cc after all, and not the slightly bigger lump. Finally, there was a small hole in the windscreen, presumably drilled at some point in the car's past for taking a thin cable, maybe for a telephone.

On the plus side was the exhaust: a straight through system, it emitted a delightful howl on changing up and down.

I got stuck in: there were the brake pads to attend to (these were on back-to-front); spacers to add to the front hubs (the larger tyres were rubbing the bodywork on extreme lock – they still did afterwards, but since the MOT station fitted them in the first place, they didn't comment); and the handbrake linkage needed rebuilding. The engine was de-smogged and a new (secondhand) carburettor and needle was sourced; and some work was done on the exhaust to secure it. Not long afterwards I lost the bottom gears and the gearbox was pronounced somewhat past its sell-by date, so a reconditioned unit was fitted. That proved to be much tighter. The only breakdown occurred on the way to a car show when the Moke lost power and glided to a halt. This uncharacteristic behaviour was caused by a wire coming adrift on the ignition system. A five second job to put right—and then we were on our way again.

I didn't tend to venture out on to the motorway with my new toy (let's be honest – you're very vulnerable and in the south-east no-one drives at less than 70 mph) and on long journeys, it was tiring with the buffeting wind and noise levels. For me, with a 998cc model, it was bearable on A Roads but I'd have preferred a little more oomph that the 1275cc engine would bring. The Moke was at its best on hot days when I got a tan yet remained sublimely cool at the same time. It was habitually used for shopping, tennis and popping over to the local tip, although it did carry the entire family on occasions.

Another car that always invites comment! Emma tries her new toy for size but finds she still needs to grow a little

As most owners are aware, driving a Moke means you are the centre of attention wherever you go. Not only do you get stared at but you can upstage just about any other car on the road. Forget that convertible Aston Martin in front – it's you the public gapes at, especially if you have a brightly-coloured Moke such as this was. I met all sorts of people who were interested in it, some knowledgeable, some clueless, and I picked up odd anecdotes about other people's past experiences with these cars.

There's something about Mokes that brings out the best in people!

CHAPTER SIXTEEN

4 x flaw

1943 Ford Jeep

To use the famous Second World War film title, this vehicle turned out to be a bridge too far.

With the Moke and the Caterham you could argue that I was utterly spoiled—and in that assertion you'd be dead right. For the level of investment I felt that I had the best of all possible worlds: a quick car and a pottering car, both of which were sound and which represented unparalleled fun in the sun. But I found myself busy with so many other things (not least children), that they were getting less and less use. A remark from Helen to that effect set me thinking that perhaps I should rationalise my life and just focus on one vehicle that would answer all our needs.

I suppose, looking back, that keeping the Moke, especially after going to all the trouble of importing it, should have been my chosen path. Instead, I sold both it and the Caterham and branched out into jeep ownership.

At this point you may be forgiven for asking what on earth possessed me. Well, I'd enjoyed the Moke immensely but had decided that it was too frail for use with small children. I required something more solid, something that would be its equal in terms of fun yet which would afford the occupants a greater level of protection.

Being a writer on a variety of subjects, I cover many fairs and events each year. Kent is famous for two military fairs, namely the Military Odyssey and The War and Peace Show. Both feature much material dating from the second world war: and they always had plenty of Ford/ Willys jeeps running around or for sale. As usual, I did some homework, contacted the relevant club and located a fellow about 12 miles away who had a jeep and who kindly answered all my questions about this type of transport. More importantly, he was happy for me to drive his own jeep, which was kitted out as a Long Range Desert Group vehicle. It's a strange thing about jeeps: on television and at the cinema they look quite small next to all that serious, noisy armour but out on an English A road, they take on gigantic proportions, an illusion possibly magnified by the fact that they are all left hand drive and usually carry wartime impedimenta. His was no exception, being liberally covered with spare fuel cans—and a Browning 303. You try arguing over a parking place with another vehicle when it's bristling with a machine gun or two.

Giant of the road? It might look small on the box but out on the British highway the jeep has an awful lot of presence

Well, I came away from that drive quite sure that this was the car for me. There's a few dealers in jeeps scattered around the UK and, more important still, there's an amazing spares back-up. Since these vehicles were also made under licence by the French company Hotchkiss well into the 1960s, and remained essentially faithful to the US product, so there has been plenty of demand for bits and pieces. You can, literally, build a car from parts if you feel so inclined.

130

Coincidentally, our holiday base in northern France put me within an hour or so of Lys Tout Terrain, a father and son-run army surplus vehicle depot at Therouanne, which is not too far from St Omer. They always have WW2 and the later Hotchkiss jeeps for sale, since thousands have been sold to the French army over the years. You can buy one *dans son jus* (ie as found, so needing light restoration) or an example that has been through their workshops, and entirely revamped: the choice is yours, and so it all boils down to a question of budget. A big plus is that you can buy a jeep there and actually drive it back to the UK without much of a problem.

Hotchkiss examples may be less pure than the Ford or Willys but have the advantage of being slightly more affordable; you also get a bigger battery, which is no bad thing. Aside from vinyl seat coverings and different tyres, to the untrained eye there isn't a lot to differentiate the French product from that of the US armed forces.

I drove a French example on site, aided and abetted by my offspring, who seemed delighted with the vehicle. Also for sale at the time were troop carriers, ambulances—and an AMX tank.

With 2.2 litres of low torque lugging power under its bonnet, the 1940s jeep is, quite literally, a vehicle that can go anywhere – and it will still upstage most modern off-roaders

Back home, though, a useful, Internet-based facility feeds both buyers and sellers of military surplus and it was via this site that I tracked down a local enthusiast to whom jeeps were pretty much a way of life. Well, he had about ten in his garage, along with trailers and a couple of WW2 motorbikes and racks of spare parts. And a newly restored Ford variety, with a Hotchkiss engine, was currently for sale.

I have to admit that buying a jeep isn't for everyone. For a start, they don't have heaters. They don't have doors, carpet, roll bars or in-car entertainment either. (But then again neither do many Mokes, you can argue). They also have the steering wheel on the wrong side, muster just three forward gear ratios and aren't particularly rapid. They don't fit in the average-sized garage because their hood is too tall. And they gulp petrol through a 2.2-litre engine. But you *do* get four seats, a lofty view and a rock solid, easy-to-work-on vehicle that will literally go anywhere. You also get an amazing degree of road presence: witness the Land Rovers and Shoguns that move quickly out of your way as you approach, weaving slightly from left to right as you grip the huge, thin metal steering wheel. No-one wants to get too close to those angle iron bumpers.

Fully kitted out, this 1943 experience was ready to go into battle. Note the M3 carbine holder atop the dashboard

During ownership, I lapped up wartime propaganda films in which jeeps were subjected to all sorts of arduous punishment, like being driven over corrugated roads, left outside in arctic conditions and driven whilst virtually underwater. (This latter feat is achieved by carefully encasing all the delicate engine parts in asbestos paste (!) prior to immersing the vehicle in three feet of water. The idea was dreamed up to enable these vehicles to leave landing craft during beach invasions).

The jeep was also a very clever bit of design. The headlights, for example, are actually mounted on brackets so that they can swivel backwards to illuminate the engine bay if you fancy a spot of late night tinkering. The rear seat arrangement folds down flat, thus increasing the load space. And there's a hand throttle, so you could drive the jeep without the use of your legs, although I'm not sure quite why you'd want to do this.

Incredible all-round vision and simple controls make driving the Ford/ Willys jeep child's play, even though it's only available in left hand drive format

Anyhow, having a 1943 jeep does tend to single you out from the crowd. Assuming it's got the obligatory US markings (this sort of transport looks strangely naked without it), then it's quickly spotted in the supermarket car park. Add a 20 foot high radio antennae to the rear and you'll see it for miles, assuming you don't electrocute yourself first on any overhead cables.

Sadly, a couple of months with the jeep in the heart of winter put me off the thing. Yes, in the heat of the summer with the windscreen down, I'm sure a jeep is a hoot and a half. But erecting or taking down the canvas hood is a chore (and it's easy to scratch the paintwork doing this); the seats (canvas again) repay those with replete buttocks rather than those with a racing snake physique; and the absence of any useful stowage area inside means that you can't keep anything at all in the car.

So I sold it.

But not for me! My love affair with 1940s hardware was, in retrospect, merely A Brief Encounter

CHAPTER SEVENTEEN

Flying lessons

2006 Westfield X1

After the jeep headed north to Derbyshire I was immensely relieved, for I had visions of being stuck with a LHD hybrid that no-one really wanted. I should have known better: there are, out there in that big car marketplace, other people like myself to whom condition is perhaps more critical than originality. The Ford/ Hotchkiss had been mint—just like the day a jeep came out of the factory all those years back. The new owner was delighted with his purchase and that left me in a quandary: I didn't know what to buy next.

You see, I had by now sampled just about everything that I'd ever admired. And, as was obvious from the Caterham saga, I was regressing and beginning to replicate past ownership situations.

It was a worrying time.

I toyed with the idea of another Ginetta G15 but realised that I would miss the open-air element. MGs, Triumphs, Sunbeams and even the Metropolitan (again!) were all considered but dismissed since they lacked that certain something that I couldn't quite pin down. I looked into beach buggies, too, having driven one at a show. Their (usual) wild metalflake paintwork really tempted me but I still couldn't escape the fact that driving one was akin to sitting in bath tub. I'd done the Lotus thing, of course, but I kept being drawn back to the Norfolk concept, simply because the manufacturer made such beautiful cars.

And then, by chance, browsing on E-bay one day, I came across a Westfield X1 brochure for sale. I wasn't aware that Westfield had the X1 back in production for it was a product of the 1970s and I'd only occasionally seen one for sale at a dealership. They were all home-built cars during their production span then, and varied enormously in quality: some were built on a shoestring whilst others were well put together. The run was short-lived, though, and a hiatus appeared. However, after a couple of decades, the Birmingham-based enterprise had decided to produce a second, limited run of kits, presumably to satiate repeated requests from a new wave of would-be owners.

Years ago I'd toyed with the idea an X1, which was essentially a copy of the streamlined Lotus X1 of 1956, but dismissed it on terms of cost (they were never cheap) and originality (well, they were a replica, right? The original's bodywork was aluminium and the Westfield was fibreglass, which put me off). Time mellows one's prejudices, though, and now I found myself considering this highly impractical mode of transport. A call to the company confirmed that they had a few bodies left from the run and the fact that I'd still have to source MG parts and build the thing myself. That was beyond me but they put me in touch with a chap named Jim Bickley, an aviation engineer, who'd built several of these cars for customers. I was interested enough to go and visit him and there was able to sample another car, which was ready for delivery.

A gorgeous combination of curves and aerodynamic efficiency, it seems hard to believe today that this type of vehicle was first glimpsed on the roads back in the 1950s

I need hardly add that this low-slung *bolide* from the 1950s returned me to his garage with a grin on my face, despite the freezing cold weather. We talked about specification, engine carburation and other odds and ends over a coffee. Jim could supply the car to me in Kent, ready built. I didn't need to think about anything but the interminable wait that was coming.

The idea of having an X1 was possibly prompted by a sub-conscious memory of that interview with Frank Costin mentioned in an earlier chapter. Ex-de Havilland, Frank had been drafted into design work for Lotus by Colin Chapman, who used his aircraft skills to streamline the X1's bodywork and smooth off the underside to give a degree of what we now call ground effect.

The car was fitted with a tiny powerplant, typically 1100cc or 1300cc, in an attempt to take on the French in the small engine stakes. In this the model was amazingly successful and was arguably Lotus's best ever sports racer.

If you enjoy driving something that has about three inches of ground clearance, which involves pre-plotting any routes for fear of sleeping policemen and which enables you to read Mini tyre speed ratings, then the X1 is for you. You need a cagoul (there's no roof) and a sense of humour, as well as a lot of patience, since everyone, simply everyone, asks questions about the car.

At the time of writing I still have the car, although I confess to being tempted a while back to disposing of her (I know, I know – lunacy!) and rejoining the ranks of the Caterham 7 owners. But I kept my nerve and I'm glad I did. She might be terribly impractical and really only a "high days and holidays" car, but once I get behind that thin, red-rimmed wheel, I'm taken back to a different era. I love the sundry mechanical noises, the fact that you don't get blown to bits at speed (the shape is extremely efficient at cutting through the air) and the lack of frills. I mean, there's no heater – but once that engine warms up, the wide transmission tunnel helps enhance your body temperature. That miniscule engine (I've an overbored MG Midget example), coupled with a single Weber is the epitome of minimalism. The white racing circles are not just there for effect but to (hopefully) show other road users that there's a car behind them: I never get too close because, quite simply, the car's profile disappears under their rear bumper . . .

Proof, as if it were needed, that flowing bodywork and graceful lines are not the sole preserve of the computer age. The original X1 proved almost unbeatable on the track in its heyday

I've only had one real incident with the X1 in the time that I've been driving her. It occurred about a mile from home when I drove over what I took to be nothing more than an upended cigarette packet in the middle of the road.

Big mistake.

The fag packet actually turned out to be a cast iron inspection cover, about 5 inches square, which some passing motorist had flipped up so that it sat half-out of its recess. In anything else I wouldn't have felt a thing. But because the X1 has so little ground clearance, the sums didn't add up. In fact, the fag packet subtracted from the spaceframe the inverted steel hoop that protects the gear linkage, carved a dent in one of rear aluminium trays and managed to twist the engine mounts into the bargain. It also made one heck of a noise whilst the split second passed in which this all happened. Luckily the car was still drivable and I subsequently had it trailered back to the Westfield factory in the Midlands for remedial work. Naturally, the local county council didn't want to know and the insurance company was left to pick up the bill.

Three years into ownership the battery died. It's a gel affair, quite small and neat and tucked behind the driver's seat on its side. It's also very hard to access and all you can do is attack it with a left hand. It took an hour to get the battery out, a task not aided by the near zero temperatures of the day. Contortionists, I feel, would admire this car's geometry.

The only other incident has been that of the bonnet shifting off its axis. It's held at the rear sides by four Dzus fasteners: the front has two arms that locate on a simple tubular cross member. Each arm is held on the fibreglass by three pop rivets. At speed the bonnet does fluctuate, since a lot of air is passing through the frontal orifice. However, one day, whilst approaching 70mph, the whole bonnet suddenly leaned over to the left. Closer inspection revealed that one of the arms had slipped off the tubular pipe. This was easily rectified but the problem recurred a week or so later, when again I was at speed. This time I noticed that a rivet had worked loose, enough to account for the bonnet's drunken behaviour. An hour at the local garage solved that one.

But then, such are the joys of impractical motoring.

Not for wall flowers! The X1 looks purposeful, even when at rest

CHAPTER EIGHTEEN

Historic hybrid

1975 Mini Moke

When I realised that the aching void (that was my one empty garage) wouldn't stop irritating me, I had no hesitation about what I wanted to fill it with. I was regressing (again) but the Australian Mini Moke had been heaps of fun and in a nutshell, I yearned for another. I realised, of course, that finding a second Moke wouldn't be easy if I was to adhere to the principles that had governed my first purchase: in actual fact, this was now even more problematical, for values had stiffened. What I'd originally paid for my yellow car would now only buy a car needing work; and importing from Oz, I quickly discovered, was out of the question because of appreciably higher shipping fees.

The Internet, now a refined version of all those magazines and newspaper classified columns, revealed occasional examples but again, nothing quite right surfaced. Weeks passed, then months. I went to view absolutely nothing, quite simply because there was nothing to view—or what there was, was old hat and wouldn't sell, for whatever reason. It was as if all the Mokes around had found happy, contented owners and these owners were going to hang on to their beloved little donkeys through thick and thin.

I was beginning to think that I'd have to go down another route. I visited John Lloyd in deepest Wales at M Parts, and was very impressed by what he could offer. This was essentially a made-to-measure Moke. The overall price wasn't cheap but all the bits I wanted could be accommodated. You want pink panniers? You can have them.

But cost was the bugbear here, so for a while I stopped looking for a Moke. In the event, my idea shifting the Westfield X1 proved a slow exercise. Then, fatefully, after a few months, a small, unexpected windfall occurred, which led to a renewed perusal of the small ads. Nothing had altered, though: wrecks still abounded. Or, if sympathetically restored, Mokes were priced way out of my bracket. I mean, *do* people buy English Mokes for £15,000?

As ever, an occasional rough Moke strayed into E-bay and the odd car was spotted on classic car websites. But even homegrown Runamoke didn't have anything of interest and the club website was similarly bereft.

League of Nations? Welsh rarebit was actually Australian originally but had been rebuilt in recent years on the Channel Islands with some Portuguese parts

Finally, a white Australian example surfaced on E-bay. It looked good, very good, but to my mind it wasn't quite right. For a start it was the wrong colour; it clearly sported post 1980 bodywork and yet it was a 1975 car. It had a 998cc engine (not big enough for me) and strangely, it was fitted with English front indicators. Moreover, inside, the seats were English replacements (fibreglass shells from Runamoke) and the hood was of later manufacture, since it featured zip-out windows. All in all, it seemed a bit of a hybrid.

Perhaps not too surprisingly, the car didn't sell and I forgot all about it. Some months later I chanced across it again on another classic car website. Oddly (fatefully?), this car was also in south Wales. A chat with the owner persuaded me that I needed to view this car, so yet another trip courtesy of Great Western Railways ensued. (Wonderful how you can get from Kent to Wales and back for just over £20).

Predictably, Wales was wet, but I was undeterred. The Moke shared a garage with a modern Bentley Continental, which was also for sale but the price of the latter put me off. James, the owner, was an affable chap and it transpired that he'd bought the Moke on a whim a while back. Sadly, after a couple of drives, he'd strained his back getting out and so he'd decided that the car wasn't for him.

As for the "bitsa" element, I discovered that the car had been restored on the Channel Islands for a local fellow back in 2003. By all accounts the original car had been in poor shape and what the owner had intended to be mere fettling turned out to be something of a major rebuild. Along the way new bodywork and a host of other parts had been purchased from Runamoke, as the pile of bills attested. The seats had obviously been ditched (a pity, since Moke owners know the problems revolving around finding seats, especially after two English shells recently sold on E-bay for over £250) and he couldn't explain the incorrect indicators. Aside from that, the heater was boxed in (not unattractively) and someone had gone to town with white paint. But the car was spotless underneath and in the panniers, as you'd expect with a rebuild. The engine wasn't original but had also been rebuilt. And most importantly, there were still five Sunraysia wheels on the car: those Australian wheels were getting hard to find.

Weighing up the pros and cons, I decided that this car would be a good buy, even though it fell down on all my original criteria, to wit engine, galvanisation and colour. The indicators could be sorted out; the seats I could live with, although getting in was difficult, even with the seats bolted in the fully back position. Rear seatbelts had to be sourced and the car would need to be waxoyled, so I had to budget for that, too. Other minor niggles were that the rear mudflaps had been fitted on to the bodywork and not under the arches, but they, too, could be altered. As for the engine, my local Mini specialist could help out there when time (and funds) permitted.

So, after a two year hiatus, I rejoined the Moke throng.

I picked up the car in pouring rain and transported it back home. Three days later the rain abated but the car was still wet inside – and it hadn't turned a wheel! Looking back, it hadn't been a difficult decision, really. Given that most Mokes have been customised to a degree over the last four decades (for some reason this is more prevalent in Oz), I began to warm to the hybrid character of this particular example.

To commence the car's transformation, I began with the removal of the Aussie rollbar. This was easy, involving the removal of a few captive bolts. I know that some owners might have expressed concern over the action but I stand by the fact that a) English versions never had them and b) I feel that Mokes look rather akin to mobile iron bedsteads when they're fitted.

Having removed the bar, though, the problems arise: namely, how to fill the holes. I guess that one day I'll fill them properly but as a stop-gap, a nice washer and a UNF cross headed bolt did the job. I had to get these bolts from Runamoke since no-one else seemed to stock them.

The new Moke came with a later hood that featured a zip-out rear window for extra ventilation – not that you ever need it with this sort of vehicle

Cosmetic jobs included buying a bigger heater rocker switch to fill the dash orifice; sourcing a couple of fasteners for the hood and bodywork; fitting a 12 inch steering wheel (so boy racer!) to help with entry and exit; swapping over the front indicators to Aussie ones (thanks to the club again) and making up mats for the dashboard from some black bobble material I'd found.

A few weeks later, whilst I was waiting at a junction, a lady in a silver Mitsubishi decided that she wanted a closer look at the Moke – so she ran into the back of the car. Amazingly, just a scratch on the bumper was the net result. Since the bumpers and wheels were going to require a respray anyhow, I considered myself fairly lucky.

A few miles of driving convinced me that it would also be a good move to have the mechanicals checked out. I'm lucky in that close to me is Sevenoaks Minis, a father-and-son operation, who, surprisingly, specialise in the venerable Mini. What they don't know about Minis isn't worth knowing. I was a bit concerned about a noisy "swish-swish" coming from the drive that escalated with speed; and I needed reassurance that the engine was okay. (As mentioned, it was billed as a rebuilt 998cc although somewhere in its life the car had been blessed with a 1275cc). Aside from that there was a chattering or twittering from the gear lever when in fourth.

Due inspection threw up a number of concerns, all of which put my immediate plans on hold. First, whilst the car started brilliantly, this was because of a large points gap. The engine, they averred, was not that new at all; in fact, it had been neglected for some time. The swish-swish turned out to be a wheel bearing; and the gear shift twittering was traced to the gate plate having been put on upside down and being badly positioned. Oh, and the radiator fan was mullering the radiator. Despite being an ex-English teacher and old car enthusiast, "mullering" was not a word I'd come across before. What they meant was that the fan was chafing the radiator core. Other interesting points included a bit of piston slap; a sticking choke cable and one of the headlight rims was falling off.

As I've had occasion to remark before, life's never simple, is it?

To cut a long story short, all the above points were dealt with, with the exception of the engine. This was because I had set my heart on more power and knowing now that the current 998cc was less than wonderful, I decided to bite the bullet and go for a 1300cc unit. Leyland's ill-loved Metro beckoned; I say ill-loved with some reason, for my sister ran a 1-litre car for some years and I hated it.

Advice from Sevenoaks Minis was simple: make sure you buy a car with the engine in it. This struck me as a rather complicated way to go about things. After all, E-bay was full of nicely-cleaned and painted 1300 lumps, just looking for new homes. No, they said, don't do it. Find a car. Why? Well, most of their customers who had re-engined their Minis and who'd bought just an engine had come croppers. Find a car, they said, drive it and check for smoke and jumping out of gear.

So I did.

You thought Metros were commonplace, didn't you? Well, I've news for you. They're a vanishing breed, since racers want them, as well as people like myself. If you're looking, then the donor car has to be pre-1989 (before the new generation Metro came out) and it needs to be reasonably low mileage.

There's a conundrum here, of course. Think for a moment and you'll realise that MOT failures are not much use to you (you can't legally drive them) and transporting them home will eat into your budget unless you own a low loader. If the car isn't local it's a problem. However, if it's got tax and an MOT, it's not going to be at a rock-bottom price, either. I started surfing the Net and quickly found that Friday-Ad and E-bay were useful. Amazingly, a few days after looking, a one-family-owned late Metro turned up on E-bay just 12 miles away. I went to view it (it's hard to get excited about a beige Metro, isn't it?), checked the oil, noted the red engine block (998cc cars have a buff-coloured lump) and drove it. This 48,000 miler was lovely. I offered the seller a cash price and he said he'd call me back that evening once he'd spoken to his grandfather, whose car it had been.

In the event he didn't call that night and next morning, with some five days of auction still to run, someone had put in a bid over my offer! Undeterred, I hung on to the closing minute of the auction and put in a hefty bid to secure the car. To my amazement, up came the OUTBID notice. I wasn't prepared to start haggling at what I considered an already excessive price so I left it. At least the winner got a shock with the final price realised . . .

A bit depressed, I went back to surfing. What did crop up was either off the road, 998cc-engined, 500 miles away or high mileage. Then, on Friday-Ad, I spotted a brief description of a very similar car to the one I'd missed. Incredibly, the mileage was also 40,000 odd. It was 100 miles away but, critically, was in its last couple of months of MOT and tax. Catching the train, I was soon over in Newbury to see it on a sweltering day in June. The owner picked me up and the red Metro was actually in very good nick, had a sunroof and drove beautifully. No bargaining was possible but I was happy with the price and drove it home.

Driving 100 miles in something you know little about (the car had no history but the owner had proudly pointed to the buffed-up tyres and hand-painted wheels) is a bit of an adventure as you get older. The radio didn't work; the wheels wobbled at 60 mph, indicating that tracking hadn't been high on the owner's agenda (if, indeed, he had ever attained such speeds); and the seat wasn't comfortable. I kept the speed to just under 60 and was glad of the sunroof. Bit by bit the car ate up the motorway miles and my eye, scarcely straying from the temperature gauge, began to relax a little.

Then, on the M25, we ran into an accident.

We sat, moved a few yards, and sat. This went on for 20 or so minutes, whilst the outside temperature (and that under the bonnet) rose accordingly. The needle crept around the gauge then fell back slightly, only to repeat the performance a few minutes later. Nothing like 28ºC on the M25 in a jam to test your car (and nerves), eh? To its credit, though, the Metro coped.

Later than anticipated, I dropped it off at Sevenoaks Minis and left it to them; two days later the Moke was benefitting from more bhp and the Metro was scrap. I didn't shed a tear but nonetheless was pleased with Leyland's engineering of two decades back.

Replacement 1275cc engine was fitted: better breathing facilities also helped to improve the Moke's rather lacklustre performance

If you're wondering whether a change to 1300cc was a worthwhile move, let me put your mind at rest. That extra 300cc is amazing: torque is greatly improved and the car is much smoother to drive. Top speed is largely incidental but the car was no longer gasping on hills. In fact, it can go at a surprising lick, if you push it. A secondhand alloy rocker cover, filler cap and T bolts (again from that Internet flea market) set it all off.

A Moke with 1300cc under the bonnet certainly made a welcome difference to the car, of that there was no question. Anyone contemplating an engine change will have no regrets at all: after all, the vehicle was fitted with this kind of power at one time, so it's not quite the same as, say, stuffing an Impreza engine into a Morris Minor. (Not quite sure why you'd want to do that, anyhow . . .)

But, with the car running much better and able to sprint away from the red lights (although not quite in the Mercedes McLaren league), it quickly became clear that the rest of the equation had to be attended to. The new engine really needed a manifold and decent exhaust to be perfectly happy, since the pea shooter pipe was somewhat inadequate. Sevenoaks Minis said that they could fabricate something suitable that would add 10-15bhp, so I made a mental note.

A few weeks later the bracket locating the tail pipe parted company with the subframe so it was time to take a closer look at the exhaust system. Sevenoaks Minis was duly contacted.

So . . . in went the Moke again. Funnily enough, in the engineering shop next to the Mini place there was a chap selling an almost new twin rear exhaust section in stainless steel off a VW Golf GTI. It looked quite superb—but would have been a touch over-the-top for the Moke. Anyhow, Andy and Sean at Sevenoaks Minis decided to take the old exhaust as a pattern and fabricate the new one using an RC40. To their credit, the team did know a bit about Mokes and that awkwardly-sited gearbox, since they'd worked on my last car; however, the actual cutting and shutting of the new system was more than they had bargained for. The downpipe for the manifold was too short for starters, so that to be extended with a sleeve. The idea of the RC40 was also dropped because of space restrictions in the engine bay; instead, they opted for a Maniflow system. Really, the only fiddly area (as most Mokers will know) is around the gearbox but this was successfully sorted out. They did admit afterwards, though, that they had come close to arson during the operation.

Further, because there was so little space under the bonnet once the Metro lump and new manifold were in, the original Metro air filter housing could no longer be accommodated: a smaller Mini version was duly substituted and its intake suitably modified.

When I went along to pick up the car, I was hoping for something like the noise a wide boy's Vauxhall Corsa makes: you know, the one with a tuned baked bean can protruding from under a cut-out in the rear bumper. Alas, no, it was all rather more subdued: deeper, yes, but fairly quiet all the same. Maybe I should have invested in a Cherry Bomb instead? Not sure if they're legal, though.

Whilst the car was in for this work I had decided that another important job could be sorted out at the same time: a seat change. Of course, the Aussie car had come with a full complement of seats but they were not of the correct type, being English pads attached to fibreglass replica English seat shells. I was finding that even on short journeys my back was aching because of the lack of support (and dare I say it, because I'm not as young as I used to be).

Correct Australian seats *are* out there: more precisely, they're in Oz. The Australian company I contacted could supply them, brand new, in any colour but the cost of carriage really killed any potential deal. So I started to look around closer to home. The chance of a set turning up on E-bay or in the club classifieds was remote in the extreme, I felt. Then, after watching my favourite Moke film, The Jokers (yet again), I spotted something in Michael Crawford's car. Yes! I began to consider that time-honoured stand-by: buckets. Scouring all my back issues of the club magazine I found some cars thus fitted but couldn't track down owners. A club member had a set for sale, I knew, so I called him – only to find that he'd just sold them to another delighted Moker.

Back to square one, or rather the Internet. Several companies supply bucket seats but they can be very costly. Also, I had to know if they would actually fit a Moke. After searching around I finally got in touch with Mick Holt at Mini Sport, the company that retails Chinese Moke bits. Yes, he had buckets; yes, he could measure them. More conversations followed because they seemed to be too wide for the Moke. Then I started to wonder whether I was simply going to replicate the problem of a stiff back with a more stylish seat. Fate led me by the hand at this juncture to the new Chinese seats. These were upright (good); had headrests (even better); could be slid back and forwards (wonderful – I was getting a bit like a Strictly Come Dancing contestant, with my shimmying two-step that was necessary to get around the steering column); and of course, they fitted the Moke (excellent). I duly ordered a set.

And waited.

Well, they do come on a slow boat from China, you know.

Anyhow, the boat finally came in and a few days later a complete set was sitting in two boxes at Sevenoaks Minis. Andy and Sean got to work on what was going to be a straightforward job: take the old ones out and slot in the new ones.

I should have known better.

And so should they.

Anyone who's contemplating this swap would do well to realise that the locating holes for the seats and runners don't necessarily line up when it comes to fitting the new to the pre-existing. So the pair cheerfully set about drilling some new holes. But then they found that the seats in question didn't seem to have their location fixings evenly spaced. They got there in the end but the words "skew-whiff" were mentioned when I came to pay the bill. According to Mini Sport, Mick hadn't come across this difficulty before – so maybe mine were a rogue set.

Whilst the seats were being swapped I did the time-honoured thing and put the old pads and shells on E-bay. I knew from past experience that they would sell but it was a pleasant surprise to see them go higher—and higher. A Dutch enthusiast duly secured the pads whilst a local chap was delighted to have won the shells. Moreover, the monies accruing easily paid for the new seats and left me with some useful pocket money into the bargain.

With engine, seats, interior, wheels and bumpers all sorted out, the Moke is now quite simply the best four-seater fun on four wheels – bar none

Other jobs since then have been minor. The plastic air filter arrangement was swapped for a more stylish (and slightly more efficient) chromed cone type: fitting this in the confines of the engine bay necessitates locating a Metro Turbo manifold section but again, the Internet came to my rescue with a secondhand example. Other than that, I've now had the wheels and bumpers resprayed by a local garage, Alba Transport, to complete the job.

The results were stunning but the wheels required five coats of primer after having been shotblasted by Spit 'n' Polish. As I write, there's nothing to add: the car passed its second MOT with some play in the steering rack noted, and that's been it. That problem is going to niggle me, I know, because replacement racks, by all accounts, are less than wonderful.

Again, I suppose, it's something to do with the joys of running old cars. And that, dear reader, brings me up to date.

An exercise in squares and rectangles, the Moke's utilitarian character is well illustrated in this overhead shot

POSTSCRIPT

All the cars detailed in this book have, to my way of thinking, without exception, been enormous fun to have tracked down and owned. I've not mentioned the many bread and butter cars that have accompanied my specialist acquisitions, for they have no place here. As for the cars that have passed through my hands, it would be invidious to single any one out for special praise: each has been interesting in different ways.

I haven't regretted selling any of them, either. I look upon ownership of such vehicles as a sort of custodianship and I've passed them on to, hopefully, equally enthusiastic new owners.

My years writing on cars, both old and new, have afforded me glimpses of many other classic vehicles, so I feel that I have a reasonably rounded outlook overall. Ferrari's svelte 308, the powerful Maserati Merak and Lamborghini's jaw-dropping Countach and Espada have all been sampled; I've tried Cobra, Ford GT40 and Jaguar D-type replicas, too. A long while ago I managed a spin in an Elva; I once got behind the wheel of Fiat's (now rare) X1/9 and I've even commandeered a Rolls Royce. A scary experience in France saw me trying to master a 1930s Bugatti Type 35, the value of which I could only guess at, whilst at the other end of the spectrum I've driven a Lada Riva. This is apart from the humdrum Fords, Vauxhalls, Rovers, Mercedes, BMWs *et al.*

My current daily transport is also not what you'd term mainstream, either: it's a 2006 Smart Roadster. Only made for a couple of years, the Roadster (and its sister, the Roadster Coupe), were essentially a flop for Mercedes and Swatch because the enterprises moved away from the brilliant For Two concept and swam into deeper water when they encountered the realities of the ragtop market. But for me, it's most entertaining to drive something like this, the engine of which is the tiniest I've ever had in a car yet one which, thanks to six speeds and a turbo, means it's no slouch. Lightweight, mid-engined, supremely comfortable and with astonishing cornering capabilities, it's up there with all those plastic cars I've coveted in my time. It's a sort of Ginetta G15 for the 21st century, I suppose you could say. Its scarcity, coupled to the fact that it didn't sell too well in a marketplace dominated by more conventional soft-tops will mean, I'm sure, that in years to come it will be collectable.

Watch this space . . .

Charles, aged 2, gets a taste of what's to come at his first Beaulieu Autojumble

Lightning Source UK Ltd.
Milton Keynes UK
20 August 2010

158739UK00001B/100/P